Mo's
At the Waterfront

Tradition Turned Legend

Cindy McEntee

Distributed by
Book Publishers Network
Bothell, Washington

Original cover art by Tom Alen, Corvalis, Oregon
Cover design by Page 3 Publication Designs
Text design by Sheryl Mehary

BestSeller Books
Wilsonville, Oregon

Dedication

In memory of Granny.

Yaquina Bay Bridge in the moonlight.

Acknowledgments

*T*he sources to which I am indebted for published information about my Granny, Mo Niemi, are many and gave me glimpses of the "public Mo" which stirred memories for me when I compiled the list. So, thanks to all of you who wrote about her, photographed her, and captured, I hope for yourselves, memories of her enthusiasm for the life she lived: Newport Chamber of Commerce; Department of Tourism, State of Oregon; Molly Wouler of the *Oregonian* Staff; Joyce DeMonin, from *Northwest Women in Business; Auto Week;* to the writers of *Yaquina Bay 1778–1978,* sponsored by the *Lincoln County Comprehensive Youth Program,* Lincoln County Historical Society; *Small Business 2001 and Beyond:* a web odyssey, published by the United States Small Business Administration; Lynn Jeffress, *Bayfront Magazine; Portland Tribune; Travelhost of Portland;* Early Deane, *Oregonian* Staff; *Newport News-Times;* Ron Cowan, *Statesmen-Journal*; Bill Hall, *Newport News-Times,* Shelley Burrell, *Capitol Journal.* There are many others who contributed personal anecdotes about Mo and Newport, which to many were inseparable identities as long as she lived. Thanks to all of you who may not be acknowledged, but you know who you are. Stop in at Mo's for a bowl of chowder!

Strolling on Newport's docks today.

Preface

*T*he story of Mo's is very much the story of Newport, Oregon. Mo Niemi, the founder of the popular Mo's restaurant chain on the Oregon Coast, would have been successful at any enterprise, for she represented the qualities of independence, strong individualism, humor and hard work which have characterized every successful Oregon entrepreneur.

Mo became the voice of Newport, the coastal town she adopted in 1942 and which adopted her. She became famous for a clam chowder recipe that became a favorite of such personalities as Robert Kennedy, Paul Newman, Joanne Woodward, Henry Fonda, Richard Jaeckel, wives of western governors and their spouses, visitors from every state in the nation and from Europe, China and South America.

All were delighted with the lusty welcome from Mo, including the woman who drove her car accidentally into Mo's first restaurant on the Newport waterfront demolishing the front wall facing Bay Boulevard. Characteristically, Mo sympathized with the rattled driver, gave her a cup of coffee to settle her nerves, and was pleased with a painting one of her workers later made depicting the incident which patrons of the restaurant have admired for years.

Mo was not only known for the famous people she knew, but for her personal involvement in, and financial support of, projects that benefited Newport, the bay fisheries, the local and central coast economy and community attractions that helped make Newport a tourist destination.

Mostly though, I remember Mo's big heart, her purse that was always open to the needy, her irresistible enthusiasm for having fun and her grand appreciation for the Oregon Coast which cast a spell on her that never let go. It was her contagious love for the wind-swept last frontier that lured other people to share her dream and for hundreds of friends — more than 1,000 — who showed up at a memorial after she left us. They came to salute a "down-home woman" as flavorful and popular as her clam chowder, and as down-to-the-sea as the fisherfolk she admired.

– Jerry Frank

Yaquina Head Lighthouse.

Foreword

Sixty-two years after Mo Niemi came to Newport and started a legend that did not end with her death in 1992, her granddaughter, Cindy McEntee, received a national award from the President of the United States honoring the work ethic in which Mo so passionately believed.

Cindy is the spiritual inheritor of her grandmother's exuberance for life, her sense of humor, fairness, and her pungent philosophy of treating everyone the same, no matter what station in life he or she occupied — dishwasher, governor, fisherman, presidential nominee, senator or movie star. Mo knew them all.

Cindy did not grow up with an ambition to be in the restaurant business. She grew into it naturally. She became part of it because her grandmother, Mo, saw early in her qualities she admired and which she helped shape with love and a strong example of individualism.

Cindy began working at Mo's restaurant when she was twelve years old. "It was something Granny did, it was something I did."

And Cindy did everything. When she wasn't serving food to customers or helping with the dishes, she was cooking. When she wasn't cooking, she was baking pies. She went to work for her grandmother full time in late 1969 and began buying stock in Mo's Enterprises in 1976.

In 1987 she became sole owner of the business, and Mo retired. Who better than Cindy can tell the story of Mo's which has become an Oregon Institution?

When Mo died in 1992 it was Cindy who made certain that the personality and spirit Mo inspired in her business lived on. Granddaughter Cindy walks in Mo's shoes. She continues to support the community, contributes to the growth and prosperity of Newport and the town's service organizations — just like "Granny" did.

Asked the secret of Mo's restaurants' amazing success, Cindy said, "We're doing what Granny did; we keep the product local. We support local businesses, support our town in whatever way we can. It's being part of the community, being a good neighbor.

Mo with Cindy at four weeks old.

Chapter One

When my grandmother, Mo Niemi came to Newport, Oregon in 1942, the attraction for her — a strong-willed thirty-year old woman with two young boys — was much the same as the one that had urged earlier adventurers to the Oregon Coast 164 years before.

In 1778, what was later to be called Yaquina Bay, where the fishing town of Newport was to grow up, was known then only as "The Western Edge of an Unexplored Continent." And that was description enough to light up the imagination of westering Americans whose idea of freedom was the excitement of discovery and the challenge of living on a wild, untamed shore rich with opportunities.

One image casts the land and sea in this fashion: *Waves roll toward long beaches where sands shift with the weather and season. Reefs of black volcanic rock lurk just beneath the surface, trapping passing ships driven shoreward by storms. Looking landward, east from the ocean's horizon, rolling, broken hills rise from the water's edge to form a coastal mountain range.*

The land is covered with a solid green mist of enormous fir and spruce, alder and bent coastal pine. The bases of the trees are hidden in a thorny, impenetrable tangle of berry vines and sage. Winds sweep off the ocean, yet the tops of the trees are shrouded in fog.

Between a sandstone bluff and a series of low sand dunes there is a break where a small river empties into the ocean. It is just one of the dozens of streams that penetrate the coastline in this wet country. Sheltered from the turbulent ocean bar, the river bends to form a smooth, shallow bay and then winds more than twenty miles inland before it splits into two smaller streams. This is the land that abounds with bear, deer, otter and mink; its waters teem with life.

I learned before I was twelve that the history of Newport was sprinkled with characters as strong-willed and independent as my grandmother, Mo. It took people with the same streak of stubbornness, determination and outspokenness as she to build a colony of fishermen, loggers, railroaders and settlers.

When Mo arrived in Newport, the town was still primitive by today's standards, and people who had lived there all their lives connected in some way, to fishing or logging, had strong memories of "how things used to be."

Following are a few excerpts from that remarkable past:

- By 1898 work on the Yaquina Bay Jetty to control the flows of rivers and ocean waters was slowed when the army major in charge of construction was sent off to the Spanish American War. His absence worried citizens and a group of old Civil War veterans banded together to plan the defense of Yaquina Bay from the dastardly

Spanish. Yaquina was never attacked and the endless cycle of dredging and jetty repair was resumed.

- Newport's first jail was built for the mind-boggling sum of $38.31 in 1882.
- The first fire department was established in 1885 with an inventory of one ladder and a few rubber buckets. The next year, in 1886, twelve buckets, six helmets, a couple of axes and a 500-pound firebell were added.
- In 1902, the first cross-town telephone was hooked up.
- The first electricity supplied by generator, at night only, was connected in the same year.
- In 1912 to 1915, 522 ships sailed into Yaquina Bay to load and carry out more than 30,000 tons of lumber and produce.

Newport front in 1945.

• In 1912, the roads in and around Newport were so bad
that a publicity stunt was undertaken to attract attention
to the deplorable conditions. According to one description: "Three men made a daring auto trip from Newport
to Siletz and back. The ground was covered in blazing
speed — it took only 22 hours 14 minutes and the help
of a team of horses — to make the 46-mile journey. The
car was equipped with picks, shovels, axes and saws.
The bumper carried a windlass and hand spikes, one
long cable and a block and tackle. All the equipment
found a use before the trip was over.

"The demonstration was effective and Newport's
muddy streets were planked immediately. By 1915 the
road had been graded and was wide enough for two
teams to pass at any point. "

All in all, times were peaceful and prosperous for the
fishing town. Tourists came and camped at tent cities where
they could find all they needed, including someone to put
up the tents. Visitors stayed for a month or more and
strolled along the beaches to collect vari-colored rocks and
shells. They fished, enjoyed boat rides in the bay, perhaps
sailing to Oysterville, where one man who raised both
oysters and cows did a thriving business preparing fresh
oyster stew.

Nye Beach, over the hill from Bayfront, was a tourist
center complete with saltwater taffy concessions, agate
shops and penny arcades. There was the natatorium — a
giant building containing a heated saltwater swimming
pool, dance floor and glassed-in viewing rooms so tourists
could watch the waves in comfort. There was Dr.
Minthorn's sanitarium, furnishing saltwater baths to those

Ferry days on Yaquina Bay before the bridge.

who wanted the good doctor's attention for their complaints.

When the evening came, it was time for a stroll around the wooden promenade that followed the shoreline back to the Bayfront, or a brisk walk up the hill and over to the planked road leading down to the harbor. The Bayfront offered a number of entertainments. There was a movie house with an old one-lung gasoline engine running the projector. Since the movies were silent it didn't matter that the motor was loud. There was a fine opera house built out over the bay that offered a variety of performers. One newspaper review read:

"A delegation of Ethiopians played at the Opera House last night telling many jokes that were new to our Revolutionary fathers."

Strollers could take a moonlight dance on the bay — the band and dancers glided over the water in barges pulled by a tug. Well known entertainers occasionally played the provinces — in 1912, Kit Carson's Wild West Show appeared in Toledo, just a few miles away.

Tourists could watch local talent — crews from the life saving station at South Beach gave demonstrations of their prowess in boat-handling and life saving techniques when the weather was pleasant. Their station had been established in 1897 after a rash of shipwrecks. Seven surf men were employed. They were a fine sight in their canvas uniforms as they made a daily patrol of the beach. The station put in ten years of service before becoming incorporated into the Coast Guard Service across the bay.

The Yaquina Bay Bridge which opened on October 1, 1936, was a "Depression Era" project which was supposed to be celebrated with a big bang, but the dedication was

Yaquina Bay Bridge — March 10, 1936.

spoiled by heavy fog which prevented seaplanes from coming in. But the celebration took place anyway in the fog, with parades, the 7th Infantry and two naval destroyers that saluted the occasion with blasts from their horns.

The Yaquina Bay Bridge was one of a series of coastal bridges built by the WPA. The Golden Gate Bridge was another and until it was completed, Yaquina Bay Bridge was the longest and highest on the Pacific Coast.

During the construction of the bridge there were some accidents — one young man fell 190 feet into an uncompleted coffer dam and was killed. But as one oldtimer related, a daredevil motor cyclist revved up his Harley Davidson, and at one o'clock in the morning flashed across on a two-by-twelve plank walkway, which constituted the span at that stage of construction. He arrived safely on the other side.

On a more intriguing note, in the same period of time a local sea serpent awed the imaginations of coastal residents, when south of Newport about twenty or thirty miles, a "marine cryptid" was reported.

According to the story that mystified fishermen, housewives and loggers in Newport, a couple who insisted their names not be revealed, said that on New Year's day they were sitting on a landing about two miles south of Cape Perpetua, near a chasm in the rocky shoreline known as the Devil's Churn. The sea was stormy, gusts of wind scuffing spray from frothy wave tops, the sky grey and turbulent. From where the man and woman were storm watching about 30 feet above the crashing waves, the creature was sighted about 200 feet due west of the mouth of the Churn. It came directly toward the couple swimming slowly without any visible propelling motions, and stopped close to the entrance of the chasm, about 100 feet from the observers. It paused for about fifteen to twenty seconds. The heavy breakers did not seem to toss it around one bit. A truck came by on the highway during that time and the animal turned its head to look at it, then stared at the witnesses, again at the truck, and took off southward along the coast, moving rapidly at a speed the man estimated to be about twenty-five knots.

The couple followed the animal along the shore highway in their car. At an observation point about a mile south of the Churn, they saw it veer off from the coast and swim out to sea.

Many years later, in 1993, their description of a sea monster with a long neck, a serpent's head and a body about 60 feet long, was printed in *Sea Serpents of the Northwest,* by Paul H. LeBlond.

Whether or not the sea monster sighted on that New Years day in 1937 was real or a figment of overactive imaginations, the fact is, it added to the fascination of the Central Oregon Coast region, for the sea, then and now, is a mystery that continues to draw people to the drama of the ocean and to connect themselves to this birthplace of life.

It certainly was the scene that Mo Niemi never got her fill of for the lifetime she spent in Newport.

My grandmother, Mo, arrived in Newport, as I mentioned earlier, in 1942. That was the year when the national recovery projects of President Roosevelt, in his second term, turned the country's economy around. In that year memories were still fresh in Newport of how tough and lean it had been since 1929 when the world seemed to collapse after the New York Stock Market failed. As one laborer reminisced: "Labor was slow ... I went to work on the bridge in 1933 wheeling cement until 1936 for 45 cents an hour. They had walkways built out to where they were pouring cement; big ramps. They had a cement plant up there at the south end of the bridge that didn't shut down. It ran 24 hours a day. It stormed but they poured cement anyway. Sometimes it was so foggy that you couldn't see the way from the cement mixer to where you were going to pour."

In 1938, four years before Mo came to Newport, there was a huge surplus of crab at Yaquina Bay. This gave promoters an idea, and the Newport Crab Festival was started. It was composed of festival princesses, parades, and speeches, but the main event took place on the Bayfront where free crab was given away. In 1939, 12,000 crabs were distributed to 30,000 people attending the festival. Debris from the crab feed could be seen — and smelled — all over town for days afterward.

Tourists had plenty to do. Besides the Natatorium, and bowling alleys in Toledo and Newport, there was even a miniature golf course located right on the 'Roosevelt Highway' (later to be designated U.S. 101), in the center of the Newport business district. Built by Paul Hudson, longtime city council member, the little golf course opened in a gala ceremony with the governor of Oregon playing the first round.

Tourist money was needed badly. The lumber and shipping industries were still in a terrible slump. In the thirties labor organizations began in the shipping industry, and in May of 1934 the entire Pacific Coast was paralyzed by a longshoreman's strike. This first strike didn't affect shipping at Yaquina Bay because ships had gotten advance warning and left the port before it happened, but the lumber mills felt the impact immediately. Though that dispute was settled in a few months, shipping was stopped by another maritime strike two years later. This time 17,500 workers on the Pacific Coast were idled. The strike started late in 1936 and was not resolved until December of 1937. Many businesses up and down the coast were halted completely. In the first few months Yaquina Bay remained calm, but by fall of 1937 strikers and strike-breakers at Toledo were tense. Trains carrying lumber that the ships couldn't load were harassed. Tires were slashed and fistfights erupted. One ship, the *Margaret Schafer,* was caught at Yaquina Bay and forced to remain tied up for months. The crew was sent home.

Though the strike was eventually settled, the harbor had other problems. The government became reluctant to invest any more money in the dredging and the jetties at

Train to repair the North Jetty — 1939.

Yaquina Bay. But eventually the government was convinced to fund the completion of the jetty. Yaquina Bay received nearly half a million dollars to lengthen and repair the jetties, and another $75,000 for a new Coast Guard station. However, there were other events that were troublesome.

Nearby Toledo suffered two disastrous fires at the end of this trying decade. In 1937, the old waterfront was lost. More than ten buildings, survivors of the earliest settlement of the town, burned to the ground. In 1939, the Bittner Plug and Shingle Mill was completely destroyed. It was not insured, and it was not rebuilt.

Then the nation had a new crisis to worry about. There were reports in the newspaper of Nazi land-grabbing in Europe under the direction of a dictator who proved to be the world's most merciless fanatic. The Japanese invasion of China was another disturbing threat, and people seemed to know that the United States would again be drawn into a war.

As one resident recalled:

"I remember one time just before the war, a Jap ship came in. Men from the ship came uptown and started spreading their authority around … they'd had a breakdown. One local was a machine shop man and the Japanese wanted him to do their work before anyone else. They got out in a few days. I don't think their trouble was half as severe as they let on. What they was after was to get in here and check the bar, check the channel. That was about 1939, 1940."

"Also, in 1939, a contingent of Japanese came over here talking about reciprocal trade. The Chamber of Commerce had a group down here. They went out, sounded the Bay, looked everything over … come to find out some of them was Admirals in the Japanese Navy. There was a lot of stink about that."

At the outbreak of World War II, in 1941, it seemed that a war was just what the nation needed to boost the economy. The war provided millions of jobs to the unemployed. The logging industry came to life with a great increase as lumber was in demand for ships and barracks. Independent loggers came back from a serious decline into a roaring boom — there were small tie mills popping up all over the county, cutting railroad ties to rebuild the country's railroads for war use.

"The war," as one economist reported, "speeded up the industrialization of the west by at least twenty years ... by the middle of 1942, the three Pacific coastal states were building one-third of our nation's ships and one-fourth of its planes."

Blodgett Timber Tract August 1923.

The fishing industry jumped into production. Fish was canned for the army, and government food inspectors patrolled the fish plants. The war brought many of the plants into the twentieth century as government food regulations made them modernize their equipment.

A new fishery developed because of the war. Soupfin shark were netted in huge quantities off of Yaquina Bay for the vitamin A contained in their livers. This vitamin A was sent to Europe, where allied flyers took massive doses to enable them to see enemy planes at night. Shark livers sold for $10 a pound, and as one observer noted, "It was nothing to bring in $50,000 worth of shark liver in a load, so some of those guys got real wealthy off of it!"

Civilians who were logging, fishing or farming were not called to duty. They were needed where they were. In fact, people in those occupations were "frozen" — not allowed to change their jobs or locations until after the war.

Grandmother Mo, who later was to become one of the most celebrated — and beloved characters in Oregon — began her restaurant career in Newport by opening a diner with a friend of hers, Freddie Kent, which was called *Freddie and Mo's*. When the income from the small restaurant was not enough to support both families, Mo with another friend, Neva, started the *Hava Java*.

Finally, Mo bought out her friend, Freddie and *Mo's* became the new name. The original Mo's was established in 1946. That was the small beginning for the chain of restaurants that attracted the curious from all over the world and which employed a peak summertime work force of about 350 and wrote out an annual payroll of $3 million. In the small, simple and funky restaurants, which are Mo's

Top: Mo in front of original Mo's, Newport
Bottom: Mo and Hava Java partner Neva.

heritage, about one million bowls of clam chowder are served to visitors every year.

The first *Mo's* was opened on the waterfront at a time when her customers consisted mostly of fishermen, long-shoremen and cannery workers and just a handful of tourists. In those years, fish was not popular in local restaurants because everybody was involved in catching them, processing them or selling them for out-of-town consumption.

Mo's restaurants gradually became popular with the so-called "hippie" generation which moved into the area and made her eateries a national tourist attraction. The culture of simplicity that Mo breathed into them never changed.

By 1968, people from all over the world were coming to Newport to visit with Mo, eat her clam chowder and "jaw" about the past and the future. She became as popular as her restaurants because of her sense of humor and the joy she got out of entertaining people with good food, a relaxed atmosphere and a heck of a good time. She loved a party. And party she did.

But I'm getting ahead of myself in telling Mo's story. I should add that because her life touched so many others, it was remarkable, amusing, inspirational and is more than a story of one woman's success. I think it is a demonstration of the kind of personality, a free-wheeling spirit and character, that America seems to produce. It draws admiration because those who hear about it feel better about themselves. They feel linked to the sincerity of a genuine person who knew herself well enough to be happy and glad that she could pass on some of her enthusiasm to others.

Mo quickly became part of the community when she arrived in the coastal town of 6,000 in 1942. It was still on

Original Mo's 1960s

a 24-hour-alert from the threat of invasion from the sea by Japanese.

The attack on Pearl Harbor made the citizens of Yaquina Bay aware of their vulnerability. Blackouts were required from 1:30 A.M. to 7:45 A.M. The headlights of cars had to be blackened or covered with oilcloth, leaving only a 1" x 2" beam of light to drive with. Vehicles were made to travel in "trains," using each other's tail lights as a guide. (A favorite trick was to slow down until you could just barely see the lights ahead, and then speed up to lose the cars following you.) Before the Coast Guard took over that duty, a civilian group patrolled the beaches nightly looking for blackout violators who might be signalling Japanese ships. Civilian spotters kept watch twenty-four hours a day from the Yaquina Bay Bridge.

Those in charge, as one resident said, "figured if there were no lights, we'd be harder to find. I don't think they took into consideration that those guys were real good navigators and didn't need lights to know the position of every town along the coastline ... they managed to get from Japan over here, and they sure as hell knew where they was when they got here!"

Army troops moved into the area and were stationed where the fairgrounds stood. Twelve tanks were located there for the defense of the bay. They could often be seen on maneuver at the dunes in South Beach. The navy thought Newport needed an airfield, so they built one a couple of miles south of the bay. The Coast guard patrolled the beaches with dogs.

One keen-eyed citizen observed: "They had a kennel up on Jump-off Joe, about fifty dogs up there. Boy, were they mean! The guy would keep them on a leash and when they patrolled the beaches they always had a dog with them. The dogs were trained to scent Japanese."

After the northern coast of Oregon was shelled by a Japanese submarine, planes from Adair Air Force Base would sweep over the ocean on patrol.

"They used to come in and check the fishing boats," one fisherman noted. "They could never tell who was legitimate and who wasn't. They would fly so low that the boats wouldn't know they were there until they were right on top of them. They used to come right over our house and I swear they missed us only about that far! I was just hoping they wouldn't knock my chimney over."

At Yaquina Bay, as in the rest of the United States, support for the war was overwhelming. An inventory of women was taken to find out their working skills for wartime use. As the men went away to fight in foreign lands, jobs opened up which were filled with women supporting their families and being patriotic in the process.

Women were appointed as block wardens to coordinate defense actions. One veteran of that service remarked: "You had to go to meetings to learn about blackouts and the different kinds of bombs ... you had to keep a bucket of sand in your house for if a bomb came ... incendiary bombs. I had to make a map of all the houses on the block. They even had plans that ... if the bridge and Newport were bombed, they would evacuate the Newport people back in toward Nashville and Summit (in the Coast Range)."

The *Lincoln County Leader* ran a series of articles called "Jap Bombs of 1943" which had drawings and descriptions of bombs that the citizens might see, along with tips on how to deal with them.

There was good cause to be worried — floating Japanese mines were picked up regularly by fishing boats, even as recently as 1978. Incendiary bombs were floated on balloons into the forests of Oregon in the hope that forest fires could be started. One fishing trip ended in tragedy when a little boy picked up one of these bombs. It detonated and killed him and a number of others.

Almost everything was rationed in those days, including commodities necessary to run a restaurant. The restrictions on oil, gas and tires hurt Newport the most, since tourists could not travel as much. Homemakers saved metal and foil. The Victory Clothing Drive collected items for less fortunate people in Allied nations, especially

England, and the slogan became "Bundles for Britain." The war had such an effect on life that in 1943 the Fourth of July lost its fireworks, and children were deprived of their cap-guns in an effort to conserve explosives. Even cans of cooking fat were saved and turned in to local grocers because gunpowder could be made from the nitrates rendered from the fat.

Newport, despite the war scare, was again active and productive.

As the after-war period dawned on Newport, Mo's was a little busier as tourists began drifting in to Newport, exploring the central coast and discovering the quaint restaurant on the bayfront.

More than a hundred ships a year visited the bay in the early 1950s. Extra longshoring crews were hired to handle the constant loading of lumber freighters.

The beach south of Newport.

Yaquina Bay and C. D. Johnson's lumber mill soon caught the eye of a mammoth corporation called Georgia-Pacific. It bought the big mill and in April of 1956 announced plans to expand and invest 60 million dollars in the building of a fine new pulp mill with a 250-ton-a-day output. What excitement this created at the bay! But soon the catch appeared. Georgia-Pacific planned to release the mill's copious wastes into the Yaquina River. Local oystermen, wary after fifty years of conflict with lumber mills, convinced Georgia-Pacific to run a pipe to Newport and dump the waste directly into the ocean. From the start there were warnings of potential problems. A Newport councilman said that he had worked for twenty-seven years in an Oregon City paper mill and knew what it could do to recreational areas. He wanted official action now. Other councilmen said the system and regulations sounded satisfactory. They weren't. Mo's voice from the radio sided with the critical councilman, and as it turned out their protests proved to be prophetic.

From 1957 to 1964, Newport's beaches were marred by a thick foam that came to be known as the "glob" and a smell that made tourists cover their faces and get out of town as fast as they could. People in the tourist business, especially those owning beachfront motels, were infuriated and frightened to see their business drop off by more than half. The acrid fumes in Toledo stripped paint from houses, and the beachfront businesses were plagued by peeling paint wherever the wind flung the polluted foam.

In 1958 an official for Georgia-Pacific said that the foam would be cleared up but added, "There is no plant in the United States of our type that runs without an odor."

"It is the smell of money!" claimed some people living at the bay, but others charged that money was not a good enough excuse for fouling the beaches and the air. They complained to the State Sanitary Authority. In 1958 Georgia-Pacific was ordered by the State to stop dumping unsightly wastes into the ocean, but there was no change made. Two years later, after receiving a petition from Newport residents, the State Sanitary Authority issued an ultimatum. The only way left to clear up the situation was to reduce operations of the mill to the point that "its facilities could dispose effectively of the waste materials." A member of the Sanitary Authority had visited Agate Beach, north of the bay, and found it almost deserted. He added that he left because of the stench.

Things seemed to get better for a while. There was less seen of the glob and the horrible smell was present less often. But soon the glob returned, and in 1964, the *Newport Graphic Review* printed a full-cover picture of the viscous, smelly foam covering the beach. Finally, the State legislature was convinced that it should take action when a representative in favor of cleaning up the beaches visited a legislative meeting. He "accidentally" spilled a quart jar full of the glob that he had brought along from Newport, and the room cleared out instantly. When the awful smell subsided, Georgia-Pacific was ordered to fix things or else! A 3,000 foot extension of the sewer pipe was built and a dispersing devise was placed on the end of it, so that the glob floated out to sea.

Newport lost population during the 1960s — times were bad despite the valiant efforts of Mo on her radio show where she and other local promoters, bragged about Newport to boost optimism and tourist trade. The tourist business had been severely damaged by the pollution problem. The shipping business had slowed because the main timber mill had switched over to manufacturing pulp, and with few ships to load the longshoring crews were cut back. There was some brief excitement in 1965 when both Standard Oil and Shell Oil companies announced that they planned to use Yaquina Bay as their base for marine operations. Offshore drilling was instituted and for a few months planes and ships buzzed around the area, but in the midst of this exploration the oil-fields of Alaska were discovered and the big oil companies pulled out as quickly as they had come.

Yaquina Bay came to be considered an economically depressed area. Things were so bad that the bay became qualified for government assistance, and the Federal government poured one million dollars into Newport to help stimulate the local economy. The money was used to help construct the Marine Science Center and its research laboratories. Thousands of people now benefit from these facilities, the only cultural center that the bay can claim.

The fishing industry is still a major influence in the economy of Newport, though tourism is the steadiest benefactor that grows each year.

But, fishermen continued, in fewer numbers however, to endure the "unpredictable" cyclic nature of the trade. Yaquina Bay, always famous for its dungeness crab, still has a strong crab fishery. The season for crab runs from the first of December through August 15, but fishermen are busy long before opening day, readying their boats for the season. The boats, forty to seventy feet long on the average, must have all their gear changed as many of them have just finished shrimp or salmon season. Crab pots, wire mesh baskets which trap crab with a one-way door, are re-knitted or mended, and loaded on board. The bigger boats service 200 to 800 pots. This is quite a change from the early days when crab was fished from small skiffs in the bay that could carry only 40 or 50 pots.

The shrimp fishery is a recent one. Although shrimp have always been in the bay they had to be hand-picked when caught. Packing companies decided it wasn't a commercially feasible business because too many people had to be hired for the tedious work. It took 30 people to do the processing from one boat. In 1956, a shrimp peeling machine was invented which made it possible to process large quantities. Since then, shrimping has grown to be one of the most profitable of the fisheries. Shrimp catches have increased each year.

Fishing boat coming home at the end of the day.

My granny, Mo Niemi, was one of the farsighted business persons in Newport to understand the great natural value of the Yaquina Bay estuary and was an active member of the Yaquina Bay Economic Foundation which she supported to preserve the quality of the estuary. It was, and is, the source of life for Yaquina Bay. She knew the estuary was defined as the lower course of a river in which the river's current meets the sea's tide. The inter-relationship of fresh and salt water, tideflats, marshes and sloughs creates one of the most biologically productive environments on earth. Yaquina Bay's estuary, she and others learned, was particularly healthy, as wind and rain created excellent circulation within the bay. Natural wastes are removed and high oxygen and nutrient levels are maintained.

Inestimable is the value of the estuary because it is a sanctuary for the young of many species of fish. Herring, some salmon, perch, flounder, sole and crab — all must use the estuary to reproduce. Along with oysters, at least four species of clam and seven species of shrimp breed and live in Yaquina Bay's estuary — together with small crustaceans such as amphipods and isopods, which are a major source of food to the fish that support all of Yaquina Bay's fishing industries.

Though I never heard her put it in so many words, Mo loved the life of the fishermen and I know a description I read in the fine booklet sponsored by the Lincoln County Comprehensive Youth Program, called *Yaquina Bay 1778–1978,* caught for her the ancient pull and magnetism of the sea which drew men from all ages to fish it. When her husband, Dutch, rose early in the morning, I think these were the feelings that came over her:

Dutch on his fishing boat the 'F/V Spray'.

"It is three o'clock in the morning and your eyes don't want to open, but you have to get started. There is work to be done. You pull on your cold, salty long-johns, jeans and flannel shirt. As you head down to the bay-front, you pass land that used to be covered with trees. Skeleton frames of 2 x 4s now sprout out of the ground. During the day the streets are filled with vehicles of every imaginable sort, but now, in the early hours, it seems as if no one knew the place ever existed. The docks are silent except for the movements of other fishermen. Fog surrounds every object. The Coast Guard flags signal a small craft warning — though the bay is calm and still, it will soon be windy.

"You take the chance and decide to go out. After crossing the bar, the boat rocks its way across the waves. You feel cold, wet and alone in the dark. Soon the work will begin — work with dangerous machinery on a slippery, pitching deck. Will the equipment break down? Will you fish all day and end up with nothing? Will you collide with a log or another boat in the heavy fog? Five miles out — sun up and gear down — you pause and look back over your shoulder. The Pacific rolls in even waves to the long beaches whose sands shift with the weather and season. It is probably the sun glaring in your eyes, but for a brief second the land looks like a solid green mat of enormous fir and spruce, alder and bent coastal pine — as it once was. Blink once and it is gone."

Bill Dixon
Mo's first husband

Bill and Mo
Dixon

Mo with her two sons,
Sonny and Bill, and first
husband Bill Dixon.

Chapter Two

While I was always close to my mother, with Granny Mo I had a different relationship. My parents were protective, but Granny let me go, let me fly. I was four or five years old, when she was working at her restaurant. She let me go outside and play with my trike and I pedaled it up and down Bayfront. It was like an exotic foreign port with the bay water lapping against the wooden pilings, the screeching of seagulls, and the unforgettable smell of the ocean on every fresh breeze that ruffled my hair. I got to explore the water front with a sense of independence my parents never would have allowed.

The whole story of Mo started when she came to Newport with her parents, Leon and Beulah Kutzner. Leon and Mo went into the beer selling business at the *Bay Haven Saloon* on the corner of Bay Front Street and Fall Street. It is still there today, a Newport landmark. While Mo worked with her dad behind the bar, her husband, Bill Dixon Sr., whom I always called "Pappy," worked as a shingle weaver in a mill at Toledo, a few miles from Newport. Mo and

Pappy had lived in Sweet Home, Oregon before they moved to Newport and there Pappy earned a living as a shingle weaver while Mo stayed home and raised her two sons. The couple weren't getting along too well and things didn't improve when they came to Newport. Pappy had a drinking problem and his access to beer at the Bay Haven made it worse.

It was fortuitous that Mo met Tom and Sylvia Becker, who with their oldest child, lived in an apartment owned by Mo's parents. She was introduced to the couple by her dad, Leon and Tom hired her as a receptionist at his radio station KNPT.

Mo's job as a receptionist didn't last long, for one day — just like big show business — someone didn't show up

Mo at the microphone.

— and Tom Becker told her to go on the air. That's how her career as a restaurateur and radio commentator started.

Mo's success as a radio celebrity was because she was a spunky woman. She loved people. She was gregarious. People were drawn to her. Had she lived 50 years earlier, she would have been Cactus Kate from Arizona. Once, Granny met that notorious woman who was a whorehouse Madam with a wide open sense of humor. And she just loved her!

Granny was a lively, into-everything, interested-in-everyone-and-everything kind of person. She had strong opinions, good manners; she had been sent to elocution classes by her parents. Her mother was a school teacher and proper behavior was very important to her, and she never approved of the tavern business. Mo got all the education, manners and learned how to be a lady from her.

Before Mo was born, my great-grandparents were living in California and great-grandad was at work on the

Grand Coulee Dam. While he was gone, my great-grandmother went into labor and the baby girl, Mo was delivered. She was named Mohava (Mo for short) because she was born in the Mohave Desert of California.

Mo at 2

Mo at twenty.

Within a short time, Mo became the voice and heartbeat of Newport. She reported on who got married, who had a baby, who went on a trip, who she saw at the grocery store. People loved running into her, because they would hear their names on the air. She became the Hedda Hopper of Newport. She was a star. When she finally gave up that job, after almost thirty years, she was sixty years old. She had had quite a run and a lot of fun. When Tom Becker sold the radio station she quit. At that time she owned Jake's Supper Club, and had opened Mo's Annex on the waterfront, with a grand view of Yaquina Bay, the bridge, and the ocean meeting the horizon beyond.

As I mentioned earlier, Mo had a partner in her restaurant named Freddie Kent. When she became ill with cancer, Mo bought her out and *Freddie and Mo's* became *Mo's* with the same good honest food.

KNPT, where Mo worked, was first located on the site the Fred Meyer store occupies today. Besides advertising her own restaurant on the air, Mo did a program called

"Best Buys," an over-the-air garage sale, and a five-minute local news show appropriately titled "Moseying Around With Mo." She told *Los Angeles Times* reporter Charles Hillinger in 1972: "If somebody's sick, has an operation or dies, I get the word out. A baby is born. A divorce. Everybody and everything."

The day after the primary voting of 1972, she growled at her listeners: "Well, we oughta hear a lot less complainin' about the way things are going from now on. Only fifty percent of the registered voters turned out. Obviously, half the people around here don't care."

Mo's voice was deep and rough. She smoked prodigiously and never apologized for it, and she tried to convince herself that she was five feet eight inches tall. Bob Spangler, at KNPT, remembers the day a man rushed into the station wanting to meet that "guy on the air!"

In 1956, Mo married Kaino "Dutch" Niemi, a Finnish fisherman. Theirs was a surprising match considering that the two appeared to be exact opposites. Mo was an extrovert — she liked people, and she loved a party; Dutch preferred a quieter, and more frugal, lifestyle. Still, Mo and Dutch were a team — so much so, that in later years Dutch thought nothing of borrowing Mo's red rhinestone-studded reading glasses … it made sense to him: he could see through them, they were paid for, and he didn't believe in spending good money twice. I called my first grandfather, the one Mo left, Pappy, and Dutch was my Grandpa.

The Mo and Dutch combination worked well financially, too. In the early days, Dutch's lucrative fishing ventures aboard his *Sea Lion III* helped make ends meet at the restaurant. Later, when fishing was lean, "Mo's" kept the *Sea Lion* going.

Mo and Dutch on their wedding day.

Dutch and his fishing friends were early morning regulars at Mo's discussing the news and solving the world's problems. Mo herself might show up for the early morning gabfests — or she might not — more than likely she had been at the Rumpus Room of the old Abbey Hotel the night before, enhancing her own legend. Sonny Dixon, oldest of Mo's two sons, always enjoyed telling the story of the night Mo's "prissy" sister Mildred was in town and Mo was showing her the sights, including the Abbey's infamous bar. Excusing herself, Mildred went to use the ladies' room but soon came scurrying back, breathless. "There's a dead woman in there," she managed to gasp.

Mo strolled back, flung open the door, and kicked at a familiar body lying in temporary repose on the floor. "For Christ's sake, Edwina," she hollered, "get up!"

It was around this time that a lucky accident changed the look of Mo's restaurant. The incident involved a woman — by most accounts, not quite sober — who had parked her car just outside Mo's. In attempting to drive it away, she put the car in drive rather than reverse, running it right through the front of the cafe. A notoriously poor driver herself, Mo was sympathetic. She put an arm around the woman and

Mo down on the docks in 1960 with a friend sitting by Dutch's boat "Sea Lion III".

said, "Well, we'll just put in a garage door so we can open it and you can drive in any time, if that's what you want to do."

And to this day, the south wall of the restaurant is a garage door which, when raised in summer, makes Mo's an instant sidewalk cafe. In 1964, Mo commissioned the brother of one of her waitresses, Jan Thomas, to paint a mural on the inside of the garage door commemorating the legendary event. The result: A mythic image depicting an automobile crashing through the wall, it's startled woman driver bearing a remarkable resemblance to the late Jan Thomas!

Like its new south wall, the entire restaurant took on a new look after the episode. Mo helped make a series of tables from hatchcovers, supported by cast-iron Singer, White Rotary, and New Home sewing machine legs, circa 1900. These were pushed together in a small, close area where customers, out of necessity, sat next to each other … like it or not. It was Mo Niemi's opinion that, if you sit down next to somebody you don't know and start talking to them, pretty soon you will like them.

There are exceptions, of course. In the early seventies, after Mo had opened a second restaurant — *Mo's Annex* — across the street, she and businessman Mark Collson, with his son (once Newport mayor) Mark, Jr., were having lunch. They could easily overhear two women talking about how wonderful the Annex was. "Not like that horrible, dirty dump across the street," they opined. Finally, Mo couldn't take it anymore — she stood up and turned around.

"Excuse me," she said. "I'm Mo, and I just want you to know that the food you're eating was made in that horrible, dirty dump across the street."

Mo's Annex

And she sat down. That was Mo — she couldn't stand a snob.

Mo was utterly democratic, and that's the way she ran her restaurant. She welcomed anyone who paid her bill — including an emerging subculture, the "hippies." This was something that didn't sit well with certain of her customers who regarded long hair and a tie-dyed wardrobe as symbols hostile to the American way of life. Not so, Mo.

"Tough shit, I told those who criticized them," she said in an interview with Joyce Thompson in 1981. "They all eat, and they're good company." In this, she braved the animosity of a local publication that had labeled the waterfront "the decadent dumping ground of humanity."

But cultural wars would soon become irrelevant. The increasing popularity of Mo Niemi and her restaurants would bring Newport — and later a large portion of the Oregon coast — a flood of curious tourists. And, since legends attract legends, Mo's celebrity soon brought her in contact with noted politicians and movie stars, thereby increasing her own fame.

Mo with "Hee Haw" celebrity Archie at the restaurant.

Mo with Ruby Wilson, Jazz/Blues singer.

Cindy meets Earnest Borgnine at Mo's Annex in 1999.

About this same time the Oregon coast began to gain popularity not only for its sparkling summers and awesome views of the Pacific Ocean, but the winter storm spectacles attracted Oregonians and out-of-staters to the rugged coast.

An Associated Press writer, Gillian Flaccus, described a trip to the central coast and a portion of her story is adapted here.

From the warmth of the car, the storm looked bad enough. Blasts of wind rattled the doors every few seconds and raindrops on the windshield sounded like fistfuls of pebbles hitting the glass. Several hundred feet below, the powerful sea smashed again and again into the Devil's Punchbowl, a roofless cave carved out over millennia by storms just like this one.

"Ready?" I said, turning to my companion. On the count of three, we forced open the car doors and stepped outside, gasping as the wind snatched our breath away.

"This is awesome! This is what I call the beach," my friend screamed over the pounding surf.

A few minutes later, drenched and exhilarated, he and I headed to the next storm-watching hot spot — the Spouting Horns at Depoe Bay — where lava tubes deep in the rocks channel crashing waves into misty, 15-foot-tall geysers.

Rushing to the coast to watch winter storms has long been a peculiar pastime among Oregonians. Now it's catching on with tourists, who are showing up on Oregon's beaches months after summer vacationers have abandoned the coast.

The Devil's Punchbowl

The numbers are picking up every year and hotels offer winter storm watching packages with such romantic suggestions as "Stormy Weather Getaways" that include fireplaces, in-room whirlpools and seaside balconies. Others offer reduced winter rates, special deals that include a second night at half-price or a third night free.

The combination of big waves and the surf are a powerful thing to watch, as Mo and I learned. They change the color of the ocean — sometimes it'll be a blue-gray or a dark gray or a greenish color.

As one observer noted, "I once watched a lightning storm over the ocean. You'd see the lightning come down and hit the water and then the light came out from there, under the water. It was awesome."

Visitors are overwhelmed by the violence of the winter seas. From forested cliffs that tower over the sea, the view of the rugged Oregon Coast is beautiful any time of the year, from Astoria in the north, to Brookings in the south. Eleven lighthouses — some still functional — dot the coast from Pelican Bay to Tillamook Head. Memorials to those lost at sea stand prominently at roadside rest stops. Small towns centered on fishing, crabbing and tourism are strung like beads along the 400-mile coastline, separated by a few dozen miles of the curving U.S. 101 that faithfully traces the sea.

Each stop off the road has its own claim to fame — the smallest natural harbor in the world; the best whale watching town on the Oregon Coast, the best winter agating; or home of the aquarium that once held Keiko, the killer whale, star of the movie *Free Willy.*

Tourists, of course, who are chilled and soaked from storm watching pack into the comfort of one of Mo's seafood restaurants and warm their insides with big, steaming bowls of clam chowder and chunks of crusty bread. The restaurants always overlook the water, and they are always full, a tribute to Mo's foresight.

My granny, Mo, was always aware of people in need. In those early days of the forties there were a lot of people in need; times had been tough during the Depression. She always made certain that the people and their families who worked for her had enough to eat.

"As long as you are working here, your children and family will always eat," she said to the help whom she always treated in the same way that she wanted to be treated.

At that time she had an income from Hava Java, Mo's and from her job at the radio station.

She couldn't carry a tune in a bucket, but she used to do all sorts of dramatic things. When all the family was together on a Saturday, and we kids were hanging around her, she always did something to entertain us.

Top left to right: Sonny, Tamie, Dutch, Mo, Bill and Judy.
Bottom left to right: Kaino, Shelly, Cindy,
Tammy and Kevin.

"Granny, Granny, do Dirty Feet," we used to yell. And she would tell us a little sketch and perform like an actor. It was always the same story about a little kid whose feet got dirty even after his mama told him not to get them dirty, because he had to go to church. She told other stories, but Dirty Feet was a long and dramatic acting out and we laughed and laughed at every turn. The more we laughed the more dramatic Granny got.

One of my earliest memories was Mo's relationship with Gracie Hanson who was running for governor of Oregon. Gracie was a gregarious, outrageous woman who had worked in the Barbary Coast at the Hoyt Hotel in Portland before she decided she was smart enough to run the state. She had two-inch long eyelashes, black hair, and wore huge diamonds and red, red long fingernails. She was short, stocky and bigger than life. She did not make it as governor. She hung around Mo's the whole time she was in Newport. She and Granny really hit it off! This was in 1960 and Granny talked a lot about Gracie and her campaign for governor on the radio.

Through all the years, amid all of the people she met, Mo remained loyal to the faithful ones who worked for her. Early, when her former partner, Freddie, became ill with cancer, part of the buy out price Mo paid Freddie for her share in the restaurant was an understanding that Freddie's children agreed to keep the restaurant going until they could find better paying jobs.

"I'll tell you," Mo reflected later, "they soon found jobs where they made more money."

At the time Mo's was a 24-hour a day operation, with a full-service menu. But clam chowder — in the early 1950s, "you couldn't have given it away." The reason — all of the locals made their own.

But as Mo had long been predicting, the tourists were beginning to stream in, and they wanted seafood.

The formula for Mo's clam chowder was the product of evolution and creative competition, rather than a single stroke of genius.

Granny said that the old cooks she had working for her always insisted on the best of everything to work with. They were also jealous of each other and would hide the remains of their creations. The short-term result: spoiled leftovers.

The long-term result, however, was a world-famous product. Once Mo and customers were satisfied with her clam chowder the recipe became "written in stone."

All the clam chowder base is still manufactured at the original Mo's. It is refrigerated and delivered to the other locations twice weekly.

"Twenty-five hundred pounds of the base is produced every day," said Sonny, Mo's son, who operated the frozen food manufacturing. "Last year, over 150,000 pounds of the frozen base was sold, as far east as St. Louis."

By the late 1970s, the original Mo's, the Annex across the street and Mo's West in Otter Rock were thriving. But the opportunity for further expansion presented itself in the person of Mo's old boss, Tom Becker, who had sold station KNPT where Mo had become the voice of Newport.

Mo's West at Devil's Punch Bowl, Otter Rock, Oregon.

Mo and Becker together formed the Newport Pacific Corp., which resulted in the acquisition of Mo's Newport Pacific Oyster Farm on Yaquina Bay, and the launching of Mo's in Taft, Florence and Coos Bay.

But the original Mo's remained the heart of the business, and it was the place where many vivid memories were made.

The old building has developed some scars through the years. It lost its front not once, but twice.

The first time was during the Columbus Day storm of 1962.

I remember that the front of the building was torn off by the winds and dropped on a pickup truck across the street. My father, Sonny, picked up the wreckage and dumped it in the bay.

As I touched upon earlier, a family arrived early one morning, seeking to have their thermos jugs filled with coffee in preparation for a fishing trip.

A young boy wandered into the restaurant and informed his father that his mother wanted the car keys.

What happened moments later has been immortalized on the inside of the front of the door. The woman put the car in drive and it came "right through the front of the building, clean to the cash register."

As the emergency vehicles arrived, Mo spotted the young boy and asked him if everyone was okay. He said that they were, and informed her that the incident "Ain't nothing new. Mom done the same thing to our garage at home."

Although there have been many eventful years, Mo said the most memorable ones were when "the hippies came. They came by the hundreds; I don't know what they ever saw in Newport. And they zeroed in on Mo's. It was crazy. I was trying to figure out why they left home in the first place. They didn't trust anyone but me, apparently. I was only working 24 hours a day at the time, but I had to go to the courthouse and appear for these kids when they ran afoul of the law."

She observed the counterculture members in her straightforward way: "They were all smarter than the people prosecuting them."

Original Mos during the Hippy Days.

In the decades since then Mo watched many of the hippies settle in Newport and become involved in the community. She missed the excitement of the era, and the contributions they made to the community. "Why don't they do that now?" Mo asked rhetorically of no one in particular, "What's wrong with helping out — there are some people who do it, but there are few, who really work and and organize things."

She was always adamant that many community events could benefit from increased volunteer effort.

Her attitude about hippies of the sixties was a direct extension of her loyalty to people who worked for her and became affectionate parts of Mo's family.

One of her close friends was a woman about Mo's own age and because they had grown up in the same era they had a lot in common.

Elsie Martin was the woman who became famous baking thousands of pies for Mo's restaurants. Her story was told in the *Newport News* in December of 1981, and from it I learned more about Elsie than I ever knew as Mo's granddaughter. I've leaned on it heavily to recount the life of the woman my granny admired.

Before Elsie Martin came to Mo's, she was just 19 when she took a teaching job in the wilds of Siletz, Oregon in 1919. In those days, the trip from Portland, where she was raised, to the coastal town of Siletz, was made by trains, boats, horse drawn wagons and canoes.

"In those days," Elsie said, "you didn't need to go to college to become a teacher, you just took a state exam. Well, I passed mine and came to Siletz to teach."

She became a school marm in a one-room building, and later had other jobs, including riveting plane tails together during World War II, and working in many local restaurants, including Mo's as a pie baker for which she earned quite a reputation.

While she taught in Siletz, she boarded with a family there.

"They didn't have a bathtub and washing up consisted of taking a basin of hot water up to your room. Oh, how I longed for a real bath. But there was always the river."

Elsie recalled that the school she taught in sat on the bank of the river. "I had five little ones as students. Three Indians and two 'pohawks'. They came to school during the summer months by boat for that was when the water wasn't so high."

"I didn't have to miss baths too much, though," she remembered with a laugh. "During recess in the summer, we'd all go swimming in the creek." It was in the Siletz area that Elsie met her first husband, "a man by the name of Wheeler." He and his brother owned a sawmill in Siletz.

"In November of 1920 it rained steadily for nine days and nights. There was so much flooding that everything that sat on the river was washed away. Including the sawmill."

The family moved to Newport where Elsie bore four children. During the depression her husband, who had been out of work since the closure of his mill, traveled to eastern Oregon to find a job and money. "He never came back," Elsie recalled.

With young children to feed and support, Elsie decided to take on another job.

"I decided to start working as soon as the kids were old enough to be taken care of by a babysitter," she said. "My first job was in a cafe down on Nye Beach which sat where the turnaround parking lot is now.

"It was quite an experience. The people who owned the cafe lived on the floor above it, so when we weren't too busy with customers we were doing things like washing and mending."

She also worked in a cafe near the old Rip Tide shoe shop in town and in a cafe near where the bridge is now.

"Before the bridge, people crossed the bay by ferry," she said. "Our restaurant sat right in front of the ferry dock, so we had busy times when the ferry came in and out."

Life on the waterfront in those days was extremely exciting.

"The crowd was rough, but not too rough. Of course the men got a little rowdy and spoke gruffly, but they wouldn't hurt you."

She found watching the ships coming in fascinating and enjoyed meeting different people. Wistfully, she said, "I hate to say it but the waterfront looked so much better then. It was not so crowded and Newport wasn't at all a tourist town. There were only four fish companies on the bay front then. We often had parties at one of them. House parties were popular then, too, someone was always throwing a party at their house."

She loved the times when the man who ran the ferry would once in a while invite her for a moonlight cruise down the bay toward Toledo.

"He'd say 'Come on Elsie, let's go for a ride. I've got a couple of beers.' So I'd fix some sandwiches and off we'd go."

After an absence of about four years in Portland working in the war industries, Elsie moved back to Newport and hired on at Mo's. "I started working the graveyard shift. But I enjoyed it because the nightlife was exciting on the bayfront."

Two years of working graveyard shift paved the way for her to daytime hours.

"We didn't have a big menu then, because in the early fifties. Mo hadn't gone to specializing in seafood yet."

The menu listed hamburgers, fries, meats and potatoes, dishes the fishermen loved. "Dinner generally cost about $1.50 and we'd have a blue plate special each lunch hour for $1. It wasn't a huge meal with several courses, but it filled up the plate and the working men's stomachs."

Mo began having Elsie make pies for the cafes. "I made pies for all three of Mo's restaurants. Pretty soon, it got so I would go to work at four o'clock in the morning. just to make pies."

In her time as a pie baker at Mo's, some 20 years-plus in all, Elsie became somewhat of a bayfront legend for her pie baking. On a typical day she would make about 30 pies and on Sundays 50 or 60.

"I didn't stop working there until I was 77, and the only reason I had to quit was because of my eyesight." She had cataract surgery which left her sight weakened, but "It was good enough for her to sew my wedding dress," Cindy remembers.

"Things were so different back then.," Elsie said. "I rented a five-bedroom house for just $5 a month and we'd have keg parties up at the park near the bridge. I have never regretted the things I got to do," she said. "I had a lot of fun here in Newport.

"I sure miss the old waterfront," she sighed. "Once that bridge was built and Highway 101 was on the map, that was the end of quiet little Newport."

Bobby Kennedy visits Mo's while on the campaign trail.

Bobby Kennedy Stops at Mo's for a campaign Speach in 1968.

Pacific Studio... Newport, Ore.

Chapter Three

By the late sixties my granny Mo's reputation and her restaurants, of which she had several, were known around the world. And I was the granddaughter whom she had decided would carry on the tradition of Mo's when she no longer could. But she wasn't ready to give in at her middle fifties.

A whole new adventure began to enfold on a stormy day on the Oregon Coast on May 24, 1968. Mo's restaurant was empty except for a young boy who had just sat down and ordered a hamburger and French fries. Just as his order arrived, a police siren screamed down the street. The boy jumped up and ran outside to look, only to be collared by a secret service agent. Just then a motorcade approached. Out of a limousine stepped Robert and Ethel Kennedy who walked into Mo's leading a large crowd.

Bobby and Ethel saw the lone hamburger and French fries sitting on the table. Without asking, they sat down and began to eat. Granny Mo, who had been busy in the kitchen, came out to greet the presidential hopeful. She planned to serve clam chowder and shrimp sandwiches and her eyes widened when she saw that Bobby had started to eat the boy's lunch.

Bobby turned to Mo and said with a grin, "I was told I was going to eat clam chowder. Why did you serve a hamburger and fries to a good Catholic boy on Friday?"

Mo looked at Bobby, her hand on her hip and said with her I-have-seen-it-all, husky voice, "I didn't serve it to you. You are eating somebody else's meal."

With that everybody in the room burst into laughter and Mo mobilized the kitchen crew to feed the Kennedys and their entourage — only one-third of whom could fit into the modest chowder house.

After the meal, Ethel said to Mo, "We sure enjoyed that chowder, but I feel so sorry for the people who are outside and couldn't eat with us. Do you have 10 or 15

Mo with Ethel Kennedy during Bobby Kennedy's speech.

gallons of it that we could take on the plane with us to California?"

"Sure!" Mo answered.

While the Kennedys were escorted through the crowds to their plane, Mo mixed up five gallons of clam chowder base in a kettle so large it took two men to carry. Mo loaded up her arms with boxes of saltines and butter pats and traveled to the waiting plane.

When Mo got in the plane she told Ethel to add milk and heat up the chowder. She warned, "This will scorch if it's too hot, so you've got to continually stir it."

"I can't cook," Ethel declared. "If you want that chowder to be good, you'd better come along and fix it for us."

"Forget it," Mo said. "I'm not going to leave my business just to heat up some chowder."

"Oh, come on," Ethel pleaded gently. "We'll fly you back."

"I just can't do it. It would be great and I'd love to, but I've got to get back to work." As Mo left the plane, she was met by her friend, the Kennedy advance man in Oregon. He took Mo by the arm, looked her in the eyes and said, "Damn it, Mo, you have a chance to see history in the making. Don't turn away from it." She had regrets, but she kept on going.

A week later Bobby was dead.

As Mo watched the TV news that fateful day in June, she said to herself, "From now on, if anyone says let's go, I'm going to go," and she vowed to never let another opportunity slip by.

As I pointed out, Granny was already in her mid-fifties. But from that moment on, Mo, the lady who only owned one successful small restaurant, awoke to the limitless possibilities of life. She decided to seek out adventure and opportunity. Her first action was to open Mo's Annex, across the street from the original, to handle her recent increase in business. The cooks at Mo's were all longtime friends. Mo thought it would be fun to hold contests between them to see whose chowder sold the best. The women knocked themselves out to create the perfect combination of ingredients that would keep customers coming back for more.

The problem with the competition between the cooks was that customers would come in and ask, "Who made the chowder today?"

If the answer was, "Elsie prepared it," the reply was, "Oh, well I'll have a bowl of Elsie's chowder."

Another day Nella made the chowder, and some customer gladly ordered a bowl of Nella's chowder, adding, "but I don't want it if Elsie made it."

Everyone had a favorite: made by Florence, Elsie and Nella. The chowder we chose to standardize as "Mo's" was a combination of several, and in 1964 we created Mo's original chowder. It is the same recipe we serve in our restaurants today, ship to our home customers and sell to grocery stores and restaurants.

I was present when we decided on which recipe of Mo's chowder would be the one and only. I was cooking at the time, and training to be a pie baker. But my main job was waiting tables.

In those days we didn't sell a lot of chowder every day. I remember, we hand-cut the bacon Mo bought in huge slabs and chopped it. My brother and my cousins were potato peelers, and were paid by the bucket. Also, we used canned clams which we bought from Mike's Meat Market; Mike was the mayor of Newport at that time. Produce came from Portland, and Mo soon became a good account for her various suppliers. "The demand for chowder grew. First we made a pot every other day. Soon we made a pot everyday, then two pots a day and more and more.

It got to the point where we had six kids peeling potatoes; it became a nightmare. Finally we decided to remodel the original Mo's. The dining room remained the same, but we tore out the kitchen, built a new one and added three stories above, dedicating one whole floor to chowder-making. Since we were now using more than 6,000 pounds of spuds a week, we replaced our potato-peeling kids with automatic peeling equipment. Progress! Machines replacing humans. That's a lot of peeling.

We still peeled onions by hand which emerged shiny clean from the rivers of tears we shed. When the time came to package our chowder for consumers in 1976, we stopped using fresh onions, because we couldn't control the micro organisms, and changed to dehydrated onions. There are so many different kinds of onions from different parts of the country, and we were never too sure just which kind was available on the market. With dehydrated onions our workload was cut, and the process was enhanced since we were able to stabilize the flavor of our chowder and give it consistency. We never heard remarks about "Too strong an onion flavor" again.

The first summer after high school I spent in Hawaii. When I came back, I went to work at Mo's to earn money for college. Then push came to shove, and there was never the right time for me to leave. Granny always needed me for this or that, and commented, "You don't need to go to

Cindy at Mo's Annex during the late 1970s.

school, all you need to know about running this business you can learn right here."

Then she hired a private company to teach me restaurant management. You can actually get a degree if you complete the course. I enjoyed the management classes, but Granny got into a fight with one of the instructors because she decided their ways were full of "bullshit." Her words.

"If you ever worked a goddamned day in your life in a damned restaurant," she bellowed at the man, "you'd know different. We're not going any further with this project," she decided.

Mo at Mo's Annex during the late 1970s.

"You don't need that shit," she hammered. "All you need to know about running a business you'll learn right here, from me."

However, through the years I did attend several courses offered by the University of Oregon and Oregon

State when they became available in Newport. Granny was a strong supporter of the universities. She was also heavily involved in helping promote Oregon State University into moving into the Marine Science Center in the early 60s.

I used to get mad at Granny because I was supposed to be the successor in the business But she made everything as difficult as possible for me. She never expected as much from the others as she did from me. I think that was because the job she wanted me to learn required all my concentration.

I worked my buns off for $90 a week. When I needed a raise, it was always a battle. On the other hand Granny would turn right around and give a complete stranger $500 to start up a business. I'd get miffed when she treated her other grandchildren much more differently than me. But I got over my mad quickly because I knew she had a plan and she wanted me to follow it, no matter how hard it was.

I thought about her treatment of me a lot and knew she loved me. I decided she was training me in her own way to take over some day. In order to get a raise, it would take my husband, Bruce, to go to her house and demand that she be reasonable. She'd get really furious, and finally give in. Then she'd come down to the joint and chew me out, and refuse to talk to me for two weeks. It was kind of like getting a pardon from punishment after two weeks.

My kids learned early how Mo was, and they saw what she expected of me. She knew how hard and dedicated you had to be to work so that those who work for you respected you.

For $90 a week, I worked 12 hours a day, six or seven days a week. I'd go to work to bake pies, and stay to close up at night. It all came down to granny's expectations of me.

But gradually, I proved myself. By hard work, loyalty and resistance to her when she knew she was unreasonable only to me, I gained her respect and approval for my business judgment. Through it all, we loved one another, even though I would have liked it better if she'd shown it more.

Mo was never shy about stating her opinion or her vision of Newport as the Number One Place to Visit in Oregon.

Newport the Friendliest. She loved the slogan and participated with Gordon McPhearson, an attorney. They promoted a bumper sticker program called *Newport is Neat!* Everyone had a sticker.

She promoted and supported any festival, any event that made sense, was fun and would bring people to Newport: the crab festival (the crab fishermen literally gave crab away to people) drew thousands of visitors.

Mo as Grand Marshal.

When that fizzled out, she was bummed out about it. She got together with other people to think about just what they could do for Newport. The group resurrected the old idea of *Loyalty Days*, which was celebrated on the first weekend in May and is still being observed. It draws huge numbers of people. Lots of vessels from all over come to the harbor including many from Canada.

Mo was instrumental in getting the now famous *Newport Wine Festival* started. This is now an annual event to which people from all over the countryside flock. It's a tradition. It is the largest festival of its kind in the United states. There is food, wine and colorful crafts and arts are displayed.

Knudson Erath Winery in the 1980s.
Marilyn Ludwig, Mo Niemi, Tamie Dixon, Cindy McEntee.

Mo's son Allen "Sonny" Dixon, Cindy's dad at
Food Show.

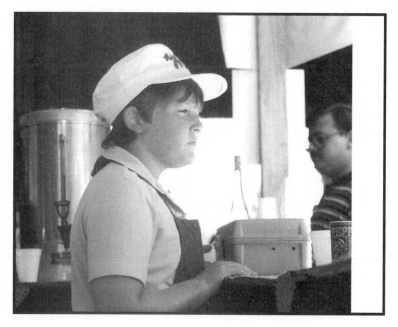

Dylan at Honeywood Winery Festival at Salem, Oregon.

The *Blessing of the Fleet* was another event Mo supported vigorously. Ministers and priests of different religions all get together at the Coast Guard Station. The boats are decorated and they parade up and down the harbor; water hoses making a fine display. Boats pass under the arcs of water from the hoses almost like a baptismal and the religious leaders bless the boats. Mo not only had her hand in this event but did the commentary because she knew all the fishermen.

Her amplified voice boomed out over the harbor as she recognized each vessel and its crew.

"Here comes Kenny Cooper's boat the *Juno;* on board are his wife and his two kids."

Mo knew the size of each boat, what they were fishing for, and commented on the size of the catches for the season.

"Here comes Dutch's boat — the *Sea Lion III.* He was the number one crabber last year."

That was followed by a reception at the Coast Guard Station which was organized by the fishermen's wives. Mo's would bring the clam chowder, other restaurants would contribute menu items and above all, the fishermen's wives would bring their favorite fish dishes. Mo helped out with another of her projects: the first *Newport Fishermen's Wives Cookbook.* Again she started a tradition which is alive to this day, as are all the others.

She was the power and the mind behind so much, and lives on in all the things she helped bring to life.

Always the ardent supporter of service clubs in town which were dedicated to attracting tourists and to raising the enthusiasm of residents for promotion activities, Mo criticized one effort for poor planning.

The event was the booking of a magician-hypnotist whose appearance would raise funds for a worthy civic cause.

When nobody showed up, Mo's caustic remark was, "They didn't advertise the program. That's why it fell on its face."

Granny made the suggestion that the club ask the performer to stay over for a day.

She had the bright idea that if he were to hypnotize somebody in town and put that person on display in a store window it might draw a crowd.

The service club officers thought it was a great idea. There was no question, of course, who would wind up in that window. Mo.

She was hypnotized, then stretched out all day on a sofa in a furniture store window. KNPT radio station carried special bulletins about Mo being on display.

Large candelabra were placed at her head and her feet.

She couldn't move but she could hear a lot of fuzzy conversations, Granny recalled.

One oldtimer in town got concerned. He looked down at Mo, scratched his head and said: "I don't know if this is a good idea. Mo just doesn't look right. I hear sometimes if a person is put into a deep sleep it can cause lasting damage to the brain."

An ambulance from Parker Funeral Home picked up Mo that evening and drove her to the local auditorium. There, before a full house, she was set on stage, stretched out, while the magician-hypnotist did his act.

Mo finally jumped up while the magician was pulling a string of scarves out of the air, and she shouted: "For God's sake get me out of here. I have to go to the bathroom."

I remember it was in 1968 when Hollywood people arrived to scout for a movie location for the filming of *Sometimes a Great Notion.* This was Oregonian Ken Kesey's marvelous novel of the Stampers, a hard working, hard drinking, stubborn and zealously independent family of 1930s loggers who refused to bend to the wave of unionism and big forest harvesting that threatened to sweep away their way of life.

Filmed on the rugged Siletz River, about twenty miles from Newport, it was the perfect location, and Mo's, as it turned out, was the waterfront eatery made famous by the notable cast of actors.

Even before the scouts arrived, Mo knew what was going to happen. It was a lot of fun and Mo kept it under her hat. But she knew all the goings on from her inside

Scene from *Sometimes a Great Notion*
inside Bayhaven Tavern.

knowledge at the radio station. Tom Becker, her boss and friend, and Mo knew everything new that would affect Newport. They were advised of things in advance and kept their mouths shut. In spring of 1970, Paul Newman and his brother arrived with the filming crew, moved in their equipment and pretty much took over the water front. *Sometimes a Great Notion,* was shot here, on the Siletz and in Toledo.

At that time Mo already had her second restaurant, *Mo's Annex.* Mo invited the filming crew with a hearty: "Now God damn it ... when you're through filming tonight you come down to the Annex and I'll put on a big crab feed. Just come down here, and you'll get the best food you've ever eaten."

And down they came — night after night. And Mo fed them. And they partied every night. They also moseyed in during the day and loved the menu, loved the clam chowder. She got to know the Newmans, Lee Remick, Joanne Woodward, Henry Fonda, Richard Jaeckel. Jaeckel came back every year to get his hair cut. He liked the barber he'd found and everything else about Newport. Now, they don't take the time to make movies as they used to. *Sometimes a Great Notion* took just about a full year to complete. The actors, director and the crew, as well as Oregon native and author of the book, Ken Kesey, appeared at Mo's day in and day out.

The Newmans had their children with them and I babysat for them when they had their big parties. At the time I was waitressing at Mo's and I got to meet every one of the cast. Michael Sarasan, he was quite a snob. He came in for our handmade milkshakes almost every other night with his agent. He was a Hot Shot, but every one else was

super nice. Especially Henry Fonda and Paul Newman.
Henry Fonda was something else. When he came to the
Annex, he kissed all the girls who were working there. All
of Mo's old friends were working at the restaurant and they
were quite a bunch of old gals — Mo's age and older. But
they were all a giggle and agog at the attention paid to them
by such a famous actor. They just loved him. He was sweet.

Friday night was always "Oyster Night." We baked
oysters. It was quite a deal. People would line up for hours
to get their share of the fat juicy morsels. I was the fry cook
on those nights while Granny had big parties in the back
room. I would do the pie baking in the morning in that
funky little restaurant which I loved, and in the evenings she
would tell me to cook up a batch of halibut cheeks, or this
and that and bring it back to feed her guests. There were 25
or 30 people in that little back room, all drinking, partying,
laughing and carrying on, while Mo and some others sat on
25 gallon garbage cans with their legs dangling over the
rim, having one hell of a good time. She adored this kind of
life; she loved being around all of them. Mo's was basically
headquarters for the whole acting crew.

Talk about those parties. My grandmother had never
allowed the word "fail" to be in her salty vocabulary. I
remember one time when she was having this party for which
she was preparing cioppino. She was all tied up in herself and
how important she had become. This was what she told me
the next morning. I had not worked the previous night.

She sat down, lit a cigarette, had a cup of tea, "God,"
she said, "I feel just terrible today. I just feel terrible."

"Why," I asked. "What happened?"

"I just don't know how to face all those people again."

"What happened?" I asked again.

"I scorched that food. I can't believe I did that." And she started to cry.

I had never seen my grandma cry. Ever. Not even when her dad died … never.

She was beside herself with shame. No one ever complained and they all came back for her next party. But she never forgave herself. Quality was so important to her.

When word leaked out that the superstars were eating at Mo's, crowds of people swarmed on the waterfront. So many stood in line to get into Mo's tiny restaurants that police had to stand by to direct traffic.

It wasn't just the locals and tourists who came for the fun. News spread to Los Angeles that it was party-time in Newport. Other stars and celebrities came to get in on the action.

One morning Mo was walking along the waterfront and saw an open convertible with a leopard-skin interior. Inside under a couple of sleeping bags was a man and a beautiful young woman. Mo found out later it was John and Bo Derek.

One evening Mo and her husband went with some friends to a nearby little tavern to get away from all the commotion. They had just received their first drinks when a young man came up and said, "Mo, Shirley MacLaine and Pierre Salinger are at the restaurant, they want to meet you."

"Well, if they want to meet me, they can come down to the Abbey and I'll buy them a drink."

Her friend, Nick, said, "Mo, what's wrong with you? You should go down there and make those people feel welcome."

Mo wouldn't budge. So Nick high-tailed it to the restaurant and invited Shirley and Pierre down to the Abbey.

They said, "Why not?"

Mo bought the first round and the little group closed down the bar. "We were laughing and screaming and having a great time," Mo told me later.

A sense of camaraderie developed between the locals and the film crew. We had parties at the restaurant nearly every night, I remember.

"Paul Newman was just a regular dude whose kids gave him as much trouble as anybody else's would. Joanne Woodward is a real lady. Henry Fonda loved to kiss everyone," Mo laughed.

When it was time for the crew to leave, Paul Newman had become so fond of Mo's chowder that he carried two gallons of it home with him.

With the carnival atmosphere gone, Mo expected business to slow down. Funny thing was, the long lines into the restaurant remained. Customers routinely lined up over half a block to eat at Mo's.

While my granny loved the notoriety that famous people brought to Mo's, she never changed the unpretentious chalkboard sign that always welcomed visitors: "We feature Oregon's fine, fresh seafood — and a lot of nice folks stop by, so sit right down and enjoy yourselves."

The story Shelly Burrell, Salem's *Capital Journal* woman's editor wrote about Mo's in September of 1973 was published not long after the Hollywood crew had left. Part of it is excerpted here:

"The crowd gathered (at Mo's on) Tuesday for lunch … was one that had never descended upon the restaurant in all its 26-year existence.

"Mo Niemi, hostess of Mo's Annex, served lunch to the wives of the Western States Governors' Conference, and the women loved it.

"From first stepping out of their chauffeured Cadillac limousines, they were enthusiastic about lunching at Mo's.

"With good reason: It's not just any governors' conference which takes its first ladies to a colorful waterfront restaurant for luncheon. More likely, the top restaurant in the conference's immediate area entertains the women, then ends the outing with a high fashion show.

"But Audrey McCall, who tried to provide a varied activity schedule for her fellow first ladies, wanted the Oregon-hosted conference to be memorable and different.

"So in addition to having an informal brunch featuring well-known pianist George Shearing, and a cooking school spotlighting the kitchen artistry of James Beard, Audrey thought lunching at the charming and convivial Mo's would be interesting. And it was, from the welcoming Bloody Marys and Screwdrivers, to the ending Lemon Cloud Pie.

"The day was bright and sunny and the bay sparkled as the women gathered on the deck around Mo's. As a special favor to Mo, fisherman Ralph Reinertson and Mo's son, Bill Dixon, demonstrated the art of knitting a crab pot. The women watched as Ralph and Bill carefully threaded the wire through its loops.

"Newport artist Dave Fish, who had painted special driftwood pieces with pictures of Mo's for favors for the first ladies, also was on hand to visit with the crowd.

"And then there was George the Methuselah of the port waterfront felines. George, an eleven-year-old black and white cat beloved by his wharf friends sat around the deck, and licked his battered paws, while basking in the sun — and the attention of the guests.

"Mo's Annex is authentic Oregon coast, dating to 1946, when Mo Niemi opened the doors of the new restaurant.

"Mo, who recalled that Mrs. McCall approached her two months ago about, 'How would you like to entertain the governors' wives…?' said she was serving exactly what she serves to the general public."

The governors' wives dined on small bowls of her famous clam chowder, plus a crab and cheese casserole and shrimp with green bean salad.

Desert was a choice of lemon cloud or peanut butter cream pie. Who but Elsie Martin, Mo's veteran pie maker, then 73, who had produced 50 to 60 pies twice a week for Mo's during the past 25 years, had come in on her day off to make the delicious lemon cloud. Nella Follett, head baker then, whipped up the tempting peanut butter confections.

Never in a tizzy or unhinged when surprises changed the routine, Mo responded with a quick thinking solution when she learned that instead of 40 there were more people coming than the wives, staff and special guests, thirty-two additional people arrived for lunch. Mo's solution was to send about half of them out on a sightseeing cruise on the sunny bay while she turned out a duplicate lunch for the others.

Often affectionately called the "Auntie Mame" of the coast, Granny learned to entertain international dignitaries with the aplomb of a diplomat, and she taught me the trick of taking on little emergencies with a grain of salt.

Even today long after Mo has been gone from the scene, my granny's presence is still alive on the waterfront and in the homey atmosphere of her restaurants. These manage to retain the down-to-earth qualities which endeared her to the fisherman and their families from the southern border of California to the top of Alaska. And she always served really delicious food in her restaurant.

One of the reasons for Mo's enviable reputation which is still intact and growing even with her absence, was because of her tremendous diversity and her influence on me to do the same. She owned and operated Mo's Restaurants on Newport's picturesque Fisherman's Wharf, had a large interest in Newport's popular nightery, Jake's Hi Tide, worked at the local radio station, was vitally interested and active in politics, raised a family, painted, sewed, decorated and naturally cooked up a storm in her restaurants as well as for her husband, "Dutch."

I'm proud of the fact that she taught me to preserve the friendly atmosphere of Mo's restaurants, and the warmth of her personality. It is evident on the menu wall where a large blackboard still announces the day's fresh food fare as well as on the opposite wall where Mo's paintings mingle with the art works of "Angel" of Lake Oswego, high school students' canvases, and offerings from different professors from various colleges and universities throughout the world.

Then there are the two favorite tables Mo herself fashioned from hatch covers of lost ships, using in one case, as I mentioned before, old sewing machine legs as supports. If you've never seen paintings framed in driftwood or wood salvaged from an old barn, look for them at Mo's.

While waiting for your meal, you'll sit at one of the family-size picnic-style tables enjoying mugs of steaming coffee, or for the younger set, hot chocolate; and you might overhear a phone call from a fisherman's wife asking Mo or one of her willing helpers to "Tell Papa to stop by the store and pick up a loaf of bread" after he docks from a day or days of fishing along the coast.

A call could, and often did, originate from fishermen's ships anywhere from San Diego to Alaska asking Mo to deliver a message to someone ashore. Another less public blackboard is used for this.

By the mid-seventies, Granny was taking a less active role in the chowder business. She was beginning to leave the nuts and bolts of management to me, and she'd always planned it that way. I'd been working in and around the restaurant since grade school. I knew every job there was by the time I was sixteen.

With the help of my friend, John Becker, we dreamed up the idea to package chowder base and sell it frozen to retail outlets. Mo thought it was a good idea and gave me the go ahead. When we added two floors to Mo's in the late seventies, the chowder factory had a home. Today more than 10,000 pounds of frozen chowder is shipped out each month — most of it to places this side of the Mississippi — but also to countries as far away as Turkey and Japan.

With growing celebrity and the influx of tourists, Mo's menu changed and by the early seventies it was no longer a 24-hour cafe. But Granny's dedication to working men and women continues. She never forgot her original customers, the fishermen and factory workers who would eat breakfast at two or three or four in the morning, depending on their work schedules. Mo's employees were an extension of that family. It was her idea, for instance, to bring in the restaurant union because it was the cheapest way to give her workers health insurance. If one of her employees needed a car to get to work, she managed to see she got one; and no one knew the number of eyeglasses she put on her tab at the Newport Vision Center. One reporter, in 1981, highlighted Mo's generosity by calling the restaurant "a very active Savings and Loan Association."

Her heart was always centered on her favorites of all people — the fishermen. I'll never forget what she said to me one day:

"Fishermen go out with the tide. Every day it's a different hour. They've always had breakfast at my place no matter what the hour — two, three, four in the morning a great deal of the time.

"I decided I'm getting too damn old to worry about the chowder house day and night," she said explaining why she shortened the hours. The fishermen's wives groused about the change for a while, which made them get up and make breakfast for their husbands, but they got over it.

Probably, most famous of all the things she did were the trips Mo took her employees on. She loved to travel, and she did a lot of it in the seventies and eighties, making four trips around the world. She was especially taken with Hong Kong, a city she visited ten times — always staying at the same seedy *Astro Hotel,* because the triangular building jutted out into the middle of a busy market street, a place where Mo felt she was at the center of the world. It was in Hong Kong that she befriended a wily Chinese watch salesman, "Raymond," who carried a store of trinkets on the inside of his coat. He was always delighted to see "Granny Mo" when she came to town. She found people friendly all over the world. She would have made a marvelous goodwill ambassador for the U.S. Come to think of it, she was.

I traveled with Mo on many of her trips and realized there were two reasons she took people with her: she wanted everyone to see what she loved, and she refused to travel alone. My grandfather, Dutch, didn't much like the idea of gallivanting around, as he put it, but Mo always bought him a ticket. When he refused it, as he almost invariably did, she asked one of her employees to go along.

Gary Driskoll had just started cooking at Mo's in 1979 when he was suddenly whisked off to Mazatlan for a ten-day trip with Granny, myself and some others. It was an amazing experience.

Philipines — 1976
Left to right: Edna Dixon, Tamie Dixon, Judy Dixon,
Bill Dixon sonny Dixon, Mo Niemi

"We arrived on an election day," he recalled, "so there was no liquor anywhere."

"What do you mean, no booze?" Mo yelled.

"We all stayed up until midnight to be there first thing when the bars opened." Driskoll said. Mo was a great drinker, but not much of an eater. "She'd order steak and lobster, take a couple bites, then hand me the plate. I always had two dinners," he said.

Mo once took all the employees to Hawaii — nearly fifty people. And another time she arranged for several waitresses to visit Paris; each of them had to save a certain amount of money. She loved traveling with young people, on the assumption that fun things happened when they were along. And she was fearless; adventure was far more important than mere mortality. "If I'm going to get killed," she used to say, "I might as well get killed having fun."

In the Philippines, she sought out faith healers to cure her emphysema and a chronic ear infection. She brought back pictures of the seemingly miraculous operations: no instruments, no anesthesia. And she claimed to be healed. She was, in fact, so amazed by the spiritual implications of what had happened to her that she told me, "Cindy, if I wasn't so old, that would have changed my life."

I always remember nights at the restaurant when Mo came down early in the evening to be hostess. She'd say, "Cindy, give me a plate of halibut, amd some of those oysters." Then she'd pass them out to people as they stood in line waiting to eat.

"Here," she'd say, " You better try some of this."

At other times she picked people out of the crowd. "Hey, you guys want a do something fun?"

The chosen were invited to Mo's back room, a tiny area consisting of the pie baker's table, some wobbly stools, and a few sacks of potatoes. She sometimes got as many as 35 people crowded into the tiny area.

It was in this same back room that Granny entertained dignitaries such as governors Tom McCall and Neil

Goldschmidt; Senator Mark Hatfield, and representative Les AuCoin. Once, news commentator Paul Harvey walked in. "Is there a Mo here?" he asked. "I'm supposed to meet her."

Friday nights always stuck in my memory. Mo served one entree only — fresh oysters baked in the shell, 13 to the order.

"All those people stand in line, and what a mess," she said proudly. "Oyster juice from one end of the place to the other."

She would have stayed and talked to her guests all day, but she excused herself. There was the radio show and then a special luncheon she was catering for 40 senior citizens.

"It's a conference on confrontation with death at the Presbyterian Church," she told me, as she ducked out of sight into the kitchen.

Mo with her two sons Bill (left) "Sonny: (center).

Chapter Four

Mo was getting old and was not as active in the restaurants as she used to be. My heart ached for her because, like all of us, the youthful spring-time mind in her silver-haired head was still full of spunk and new ideas, but her body was running down, and she couldn't stop it.

It griped her that age made her legs ache when she climbed stairs and her breath came short when she tried to do things she was a whiz at a few years earlier. And she had a dismissive way of making light of all the energy it had always required for her and her troops to get Mo's original restaurant — and the ones that came after — open and ready for the public on any day of the week.

Picture this: It is the scene that always comes into my mind when I open my memory and recall a drizzly midwinter Friday on the waterfront. It is cold and drafty outside, but despite the rain the cars start drifting down onto Bay Boulevard, as though the choppy bay will suddenly calm and turn bright when the reluctant sun makes its appearance. And the sky surprises us all of the time.

It's 10 A.M. Mo's original restaurant isn't open to the public yet, but inside, it is as full as a popular truck stop with folks emptying coffee cups, filling ashtrays, swapping local gossip and trading opinions on last night's news. UPS and the mail man leave packages and letters for waterfront neighbors still abed.

I am there, taking the place that Granny filled for years, maybe not as ebullient, or wisecracking, but just as effective. Why shouldn't I be? I learned it all from her.

For me, the day's already old. The kitchen's almost ready for 11 o'clock opening; upstairs in the chowder factory, the day's batch is made and being vacuum packed for freezing. That's the new business, which, with Mo's approval, I started about 1980 as an experiment. Now, it has become a full scale operation. Folks remember Mo's chowder, just like they remember Mo's. They want it in Arizona and Texas, New York and Tokyo.

I'm amazed when I think back to those times not long after Granny started Mo's, and she let me tricycle up and down the waterfront and kept an eye on me even though she was up to her neck in the kitchen.

It all started more than fifty years ago as an open-all-night hangout for gyppo loggers and fishermen. It has grown into a restaurant fleet of coastal eateries, with the original Mo's as the flagship.

That puts me in the middle of a kind of nerve center. Every ten minutes or so I've got to answer the phone to address some detail or other of the family corporation that goes by Granny's name.

I was 30 in 1981, ran the business and had been on the payroll for 15 years. I'd done every job from dishwasher to boss. I still do.

I knew Granny couldn't last forever, even if I wanted her to. I still keep in touch with her through my memories which are as rich and fresh as yesterday. Only a person as vital as she was can leave such an indelible imprint of herself on another person.

Very early on, there developed a kinship between us that surpassed other relationships despite how hard she worked me, or maybe because of it. And that was all right. It wasn't just that I was her granddaughter, I was her good friend. We were close friends. Ours was a matriarchal family. She was the leader of the family, though Grandpa Dutch was a leader in his own way. But Granny did what she damn well pleased. She was a strong-willed German, and that was what Dutch called her: "Kraut!" And she retorted by calling him a "Goddamn Finn!"

It seemed to work out all right. After all, they were not in business together. He had his fishing world and she had hers. But, he thought that they were in business together.

He would comment that if it wasn't for him, she would have lost Mo's years ago. With that, they were off. The fur would fly, and they would get into a bell-ringing battle.

I did the books for them. I paid their personal bills. He paid the other bills with her money. Grandpa never used a penny of the money he earned. He reveled in it.

She'd yell at him, "Now damn it, Dutch, I need some money."

"How much money?" he'd grump back.

"Well, I need $10,000."

"That's a lot of money, Mo," he'd shout.

I'd just sit back and wait until they stopped fussing and fuming, so I could continue with my bookkeeping chores. But every once in a while he would pull me into their squabble. With the stub of a cold cigar in his mouth he would shake a finger at me for not siding with him.

He would fuss at her for having paid too much for a piece of property, or any other expenditure. Little did he know how well Mo invested in the "little property" for which she paid "too much," but had actually bought for next to nothing and was worth in the high six figures later on. She always won the I-told-you-so battle — hands down.

My father, mother, uncle, aunt, cousins and my husband all have done their stints at Mo's, but I was the only one to become a fixture.

It was part of my job to run interference between the corporate types, who talked profits, visions and projections, and Mo, who talked people and principles.

I wrote earlier about the time Mo hired these business consultants to come in and teach me how to run 100 restaurants by phone in just two hours a day.

They asked Granny how she knew how much money she had, and she said she went down to the bank and asked what her balance was. We always paid bills out of the till. The consultants didn't last long.

Just like the days when Granny was still here, Mo's opens around eleven, staff vacates the unmatched communal tables and real customers filter in to fill them up. When she was alive, Granny always burst in about two, coughing and smoking, a trim, smartly dressed sixty-nine-year-old with curly-permed white hair, tobacco roughened voice and the same frank, round, brown/green eyes that peer from my own face.

Her reputation as a salty raconteur was well deserved: only a few of the coarsest Anglo-Saxonisms were missing from her vocabulary.

Tamie, Sonny, Cindy
Oregon Business Magazine

I remember how she talked about the early days, when the waterfront wasn't considered a fit place for a lady. Friends of hers up on the hill would say to her, "Aren't you scared down there?"

She'd tell them, "Not half as scared as up there. Down here I know every drunk behind every bush."

Slowly, Mo's got respectable. The bankers and the uptown shopowners started coming down. Then the regulars got after her. "What the hell you trying' to do — turn this into a white collar hangout?"

Mo's never was, nor is now when she's gone, white collar, even though some fancy and famous people have eaten here. Heck, Pierre Salinger once flipped hamburgers on our kitchen grill.

Mo was always concerned about the people who labored in the kitchen and I share her feelings.

When she came in one day and discovered I had hired Jim, the fixit man, to build shelves and counters the right height for the people who actually used them, she just smiled at me as though I had just done something tremendous.

Thoughtfulness always pays off. People who worked at Mo's appreciated what she did for them. As a result, the average employee at Mo's has been here five or six years, with some twenty-five year veterans on the crew. Mo was proud too, of those who moved on. I remember her saying, "More kids who have worked here have learned that they didn't want to spend their lives being dishwashers than you'll ever know."

Even in winter, Friday night fills the tiny eatery on the waterfront to capacity. That's when Mo held court. Later, when she and I slipped up the street for a quick shot, drinks appeared magically at our table, compliments of a young friend at the bar. Greetings all round. Exclamations about my new hair style.

Our talk often turned to relationships — our menfolk — my Bruce, a carpenter, and Mo's Dutch, a retired fisherman. When Dutch came up, Mo would confide in me that she was certain he probably was stuffing his cushions with money.

"I'll have to out-live him," she ranted, going on and knowing quite well that she was just having fun — all that huffing and puffing. They loved each other. Fussing was part of their lives, it was almost as if they had adopted roles they played for entertainment.

When we went to Singapore, — Grandpa and Granny, good friend, Greta, and my cousin Shelley — I herded them around at airports, arranged for all transportation, watched out for their luggage (this was in 1984), as they fussed and fumed at each other. But I remember seeing them holding hands as they walked off a ferry at Singapore. It was the dearest sight.

Dutch and Mo getting off the ferry in Singapore.

Of course, she went first in 1992. He followed in 1994 and I swear he must have had a smirk on his face because she never did lay her hands on all "that" money.

As Mo moved closer to the end of her life, I was with her and Dutch more frequently. I liked it that way. I went shopping with Mo; we ran errands together. Sometimes we stopped for a drink and just talked. Every once in a while, she'd look at me and in a low voice, with a wistful expression shadowing her eyes, she'd say, "Damn it, I'd give anything to be your age, and do it over again. I wish I was young again!"

I wished I could have given her a refund on her life. I too, wished she were younger. She was a lot of fun. She died in 1992, leaving behind a heritage bigger and richer than her own personal history.

Mo overlooking the Bay Front and her two restaurants
from her appartment above the Rogue.

Part of that heritage was my unspoken promise (it wasn't necessary to put into words) that I would carry on the family tradition she was leaving behind.

That I did; it was my joy and my memorial to her.

The Mo's menu became more localized than ever with the acquisition by Newport Pacific Corporation of the Oregon Oyster Farms. Prior to that time, the restaurants did not have a large enough or steady enough source of local oysters. Also, the effort and commitment of the original principals in Newport Pacific, Mo and Tom, was strained because both of them were dedicated to making their original commercial ventures successful. Mo sparked Tom's initial interest in the business. "She absolutely couldn't find good dependable oysters anyplace," Becker said.

The pair invested $15,000 in the oyster research going on at the OSU Hatfield Marine Science Center, and acquired a small oyster farming operation on the south side of Yaquina Bay.

I still remember Mo, myself and the Becker family getting together in the early 1970s to string oyster shells for planting.

But before the Oregon Oyster purchase, the demand always outstripped the supply, forcing Mo's to acquire oysters from other sources, often from Tillamook County.

Our oysters are far better, I say with accurate pride.

It's nice to tell people that these are our oysters, fresh out of this bay, shucked by people who live here. The best part of having the oyster beds, is that we know they're fresh and the quality is superior. We don't order them from thousands of miles away, they're just up the bay.

The proof, of course, is in the eating, and people say our oyster stew is one of the best they've ever had. In a restaurant with a limited menu, oysters play an important part at Mo's. We serve them scalloped, barbecued, grilled and in stew.

A couple of years ago when Bayfront Brewery owner, Jack Joyce, Yaquina Bay YMCA Director, Al Jorgensen and I were casting about for a new fund-raising idea, we settled on an oyster eating contest. It was great! The event has been a big hit ever since, and why not? Oysters are bringing to the "Y" the same good fortune they brought to Mo's.

Mo's has always been a family affair and my father, Sonny Dixon, was the man in our organization who originally managed our chowder base production operation. Now, my son, Dylan, runs it.

Cindy with her dad, Sonny, on her 35th birthday.

We don't make a secret of our clam chowder recipe, but in the quantities we produce, as any good cook will tell you, it's impossible to reduce a 240-pound batch to a family-size portion and have the original taste and flavor. So, as my Dad used to say, "We'll be glad to tell you that it's a simple combination of potatoes, bacon, bacon gravy, onions, and, of course, clams."

You might even talk him into sharing the exact proportions of these ingredients. But there would still be a catch.

You just can't convert a formula like that for production on your home stovetop.

But the mass-scale production is a necessity, given the product's widespread popularity. Those ingredients go into a big steam kettle, and are stirred with a large paddle. Once it is ready, this base is poured into large stainless steel pans to cool; it is then refrigerated.

Most of our clam base goes to the six busy Mo's Restaurants along the Oregon Coast. Some of the chowder finds it way into the frozen packages now marketed in fourteen states and shipped overseas as well.

Dylan can reel off some amazing statistics. In the course of a year, Mo's will use four 40,000-pound truckloads of clams. They go through a ton of bacon a week, and up to a ton of potatoes a day.

All this is a far cry from the 1940s, when Mo began in the restaurant business on the Newport Bayfront with a vision that the day would come when Mo's clam chowder would be eaten by thousands.

Mo had some firm ideas about growth and an almost uncanny sense of what people liked when they sat down to eat. Her strong opinion proved to be accurate when she agreed with her former radio boss, Tom Becker to allow the Newport Pacific Corporation, of which she was a founder and a board member, to expand Mo's restaurants in several Oregon coast locations.

At that point, Mo already had three restaurants: Mo's Original, Mo's Annex and Mo's West. Then came her part ownership in NP. This was successful when she met a couple of people whom she really liked. One of them was Jerry Brewster who was an architect. Tom Becker brought with him the products of Becker Industries — air and water filters. Several other people invested in NP as well. Mo contributed her name and her reputation to the new company. One partner would contribute his accounting skills. Jerry brought his architectural talents. He was well connected and an outgoing person. That was the nucleus of the new company.

It would give them a bigger financial base and the opportunity to explore the oyster business. They really wanted to serve oysters. That was the part of NP that Tom really liked because he could use his air and water filters. He had a good business head and my grandmother trusted him a lot.

However, it was not in her mind that NP would open Mo's restaurants everywhere. She liked a slower pace, the small, cozy places to eat where people loved the atmosphere as much as the food. But her associates were eager, they wanted to get things going. So they bought a restaurant in Lincoln City, it seated 80 people at the time. It was funky. And that was her trademark, and she made a success of it.

Mo's in Lincoln City was a going concern. It did well. But a couple of partners all of a sudden knew more about restaurants than Mo. The next big thing was the plan to open a Mo's in Coos Bay, Oregon. They did, despite the fact that Coos Bay in 1970 was a dying town. Nothing was happening there. Why they chose Coos Bay and located the restaurant on Highway 101, instead of the harbor, near the water, which would have been a perfect setting, is anybody's guess. It didn't fly. But it took a few years before they were willing to admit that.

Then they built another Mo's in Albany, Oregon on the Willamette River. It was situated underneath the bridge, a neat location and not far from the old train station. They bought the place which was called the Noodle. It had a red caboose sitting next to it. It was a nightmare.

Each time a restaurant failed NP lost money. However, Mo's Enterprises remained safe because Mo had shrewdly insisted that they would not be a part of NP.

Actually, the second restaurant NP opened was in Florence. That one was a fair success. Florence is "cute," the waterfront is attractive, picturesque, and is a popular tourist spot. It's within easy access — on a good road — to Eugene, a busy major city and home of University of Oregon. People there love to visit Florence. The restaurant is located in a funky building on a pier with water lapping at the weathered wooden pilings

Mo never took part in the day-to-day operation of the "other" Mo's. NP still owns and operates Lincoln City and Florence, and I sit on the board, taking Mo's place when she retired. Today my daughter Gabrielle sits on the board as well.

I was only twenty-two when Mo turned the business over to me and I became an owner.

I was at home tending to my first baby, Gabrielle, when she called me on the phone and said, "I want you to buy some stock. I want you to be on the board of directors."

"Gosh, Granny," I said, "I can't even work right now."

"That's okay, you'll be working one day in the future."

"How can I pay for the stock?"

"Our attorney has written up the stock purchase. It's $63.50 a month, pretty much for the rest of your life."

She added with a big grin I could almost see over the phone, "And I'll pay you enough to cover the monthly purchase price. You'll get your regular pay check, plus the stock purchase amount, and you won't even know it has been taken out."

When I realized what Granny had done for me, my heart swelled. She had demonstrated the faith and confidence she had in me that I would follow behind her and make footprints that one day might be as lasting as hers.

Part of her challenge to me was to be involved, as she was, in the growth and development of Newport. Although she never put it in so many words, she was my example of the responsibility that all business people in a community have, an obligation to support and personally help with the development of the city that nourishes them.

Of course, Mo did more than her share. She was part of the founding group of people who organized the Yaquina Bay Economic Foundation. She was part of that, a sort of "business think tank," whose members discussed, advised, projected and dreamed of how to make Newport a better place to live. What do we need to do they asked themselves?

Grey whale breaching in the ocean west of Newport.

Mo and Tom Becker and some other members talked about having an Aquarium. There was no aquarium on the Oregon coast, and the group rightfully agreed that it would be a marvelous and appealing tourist attraction. The idea became a reality, and one day Mo roared into my office, stopped at my desk and without ceremony, in a breathless voice, dropped the load on me. "Cindy, I need a check for $20,000."

"Why?"

"Well, we're putting in an aquarium."

I wrote out a check for $20,000 and that was the beginning. A few short years later, the idea and the project gathered momentum and became a reality. At that time, I was a member of the Yaquina Bay Economic Foundation.

By that time Granny, having been behind the idea from the start, had lost interest in the project, moving on to other cultural improvement ideas.

When the Hilton Hotel came to Newport, Granny was a one-woman welcoming committee. She met one of Nick Hilton's grandsons who was here along with the head chef, the project manager and others who would serve in the new establishment. Typically, Mo wined and dined them all down at Mo's — day after day and night after night.

Nothing gave her more pleasure than playing hostess and partying alongside her happy guests. She was pleased as punch that the big-name hotel was coming in. She felt that it was a step in the right direction.

On another occasion, she beamed when Fred Meyer opened its doors, even though the building sat on the land of her former place of work, the radio station. She also served on the Port Commission when the aquarium started up.

Mo was involved in most of the major developments and major businesses that came to Newport.

I still see some changes coming to Newport. I served on the City Council for several years. I know I am not walking in Granny's footsteps, she taught me to make my own. I am comfortable being the custodian of her dreams as well as my own. Granny loved the fishing industry, and I do as well. The fishermen had, and still have, difficult times, and I so want to see fishing come back and become profitable again. Times are hard. There are so many factions involved, from politics to economics. Fishing also brought heartaches to our family. I lost my twenty-five year old brother at sea in Alaska. Granny was close to him also, and our hearts didn't mend for a long time.

Mo and Kaino, Cindy's brother lost at sea,
Friday, November 13, 1981.

Now, years later, I am fully aware of the fact that I walk in shoes like hers. Our paths are similar. Her way has become my way. Fortunately, as someone pointed out, we wear the same size shoes.

Talk about shoes. Mo and I loved shoes. No matter where we shopped, no matter what city, country or continent, we shopped for shoes. She had a real high instep; her feet were like an A-frame. On top of that, she also loved elegant shoes, even though they always hurt her feet. She may have had blisters, but we laughed about our killer shoes.

With all her wild and earthy language, she was an extraordinary gracious and caring woman. Her hospitality was only matched by the magnitude of her contributions to the growth and well being of Newport. It is fitting that my own family, Granny's great-grandchildren have become part of Mo's.

I met Bruce, my husband, during our high school years. He graduated from Newport High and I graduated from Grant High School in Portland. Bruce's father worked

Cindy and Bruce's wedding at the McEntee family home in Agate Beach, Oregon.
Left to right: Beatrice, Morrie and Evelyn McEntee,
Mo and Dutch Niemi and Tamie and Sonny Dixon.

at the radio station with Granny, and that's how we met in the summer of 1964. Granny hired him to wash dishes at Mo's. She didn't like Bruce to begin with; he wasn't good enough for me. She hated him, she didn't even talk to him. Later on, of course, she thought he was great and approved of my marrying him, saying it was her idea all along.

When Granny died, Newport responded with an avalanche of condolences; more than 1,000 people attended a memorial for her.

Of course there was grief in my heart. I had lost Granny, but I wasn't done with her, nor were a lot of other people. And that is normal, too. We all know that nobody lives forever, but when it comes to losing a loved one, all the rules change. We won't let go. And I was no different.

At the same time, there was relief. Relief that she was no longer suffering, or, as she might have put it, she was off the hook. I always felt that she questioned the fact she was still here … hanging on, in spite of it all. Daily, she had that look about her that seemed to ask, "Why am I still here? I am done." I felt as though she took off without asking me if it was okay.

It was lonely for a long time. But I feel her around me all the time. I talk to her. I was still so young when I first became really aware of her. She was my grandmother, but as time went on a bond formed between us that was different. Now, I feel that her character, her visions and her dreams have merged and blended with mine. I have become a lot like her, yet I have not lost myself. I'm still me. I just became bigger. There is always Mo. There is always Granny. She's right here.

My two children, Gabrielle and Dylan, feel the same way. Dylan was in his teens when Mo left us. Both of my kids had worked for Mo's since they were thirteen and fourteen years old. They washed dishes by hand — just like I did. We put them into the one restaurant that did not have an electric dishwasher. Now all the restaurants have automatic dishwashers. It was one of my dirty tricks on them, for I believed it was character building, not to mention sweaty, steamy, and back-aching work for peanuts.

They both started out washing and bussing. Dylan washed dishes for three years, he quit when he decided he could do better and got a job at the local market, filling bags and carrying them out to the customers' cars.

Gabrielle continued to work at Mo's, and started wait-ressing after her dishwashing stint. When she attended the University of Oregon, she was a straight 'A" student, worked in a restaurant in Eugene and taught ballet. Her BA degree was for her work in sociology and women's studies.

She is taller than I am, with the same face, but with long brown hair that makes her features dramatic. She is the outgoing, more social and people-oriented personality in our business.

When Gabrielle came to Mo's for her career it was after a three months vacation in Europe on money she had saved. She was accompanied by a boy friend she learned not to like. After coming home, she worked at several jobs. They included one with Marine Discovery Tours. She sold tickets for whale watching to tourists. I remember the day I called and said to her, "Do you want to run Mo's West?" I remember her answer. "Do you think I can do that, Mom?"

And I said, "Well, I definitely think you can do it."

Gabrielle mused later, that her mom was just as forth-right with her offer as Mo might have been.

"Just like Granny, when my mom asks her children if they will take on something she knows they can do. She wouldn't have asked me if she hadn't been confident in me. I was thrilled, because I was going to be back into something I really knew, and I had ideas about. So that was really neat. I think it is my sixth year as manager at Mo's West. When I came to Mo's I took on a management position and I've been slowly taking over other things, like keeping the customers coming.

"I instituted a customer comment program which soon was transformed into a computer file we can access to find out how we're doing. We answer a lot of the letters. On a summer day we can get 300 comments, every customer who comes in gets a card. And we read them all. They leave them at the table. A lot of people take their cards home and send them back to us with their complaints, compliments or suggestions and we act on them. We answer every card."

Gabrielle describes her brother, Dylan as the brain of Mo's Enterprises. He took an MBA degree at Westminster College in Utah and put it to use in the restaurant organization. He has become an expert at supervising department managers and planning with them on methods of becoming more efficient in the performance of various day-to-day duties. By tightening controls and improving individual performance, profits edge up. And that, Dylan told an Oregon business magazine writer who was collecting information for a feature article on Mo's, "... is one of the ways we stay ahead of competitors. Here we are, probably the oldest, or one of the oldest restaurant businesses in Oregon and it is not in our design to change an operation that has been successful for almost sixty years.

Dylan and Gabrielle
Children's Advocacy Ball.

How do we continue to do that? It's a lot of little, but very important things, as simple as unifying the advertising for all six restaurants so that one dominant message tells the story of Mo's.

"Gabrielle did that. It took a lot of work, but it pays off. Other things are important, like tightening our controls making sure we are getting all we can for the money we are spending on food. Making certain we are giving excellent customer service every time; making sure our bathrooms are clean; making certain the experience people have at Mo's is always good, pleasant and memorable. You can never be perfect. There's always something more you can do. We want to know why, if someone says, 'I'm not coming back tomorrow.' We want to know why, so we can fix it."

"Every business," Dylan said, thoughtfully, "needs a plan to replace the management. Mom replaced Mo. Now she has Gabrielle and me to replace her. This is one of the biggest challenges of the small business owner — duplicating himself, so he or she can feel free to take off from time to time. My mom had essentially duplicated herself, but in two different people, Gabrielle and me. I showed up on the scene four years ago after college. At that time I believe we had two computers. The other day I counted ten in the office. There are certain advantages we can gain through technology. The way we use our computers is extremely effective to give a day to day picture of our overall operations.

"From the programs we've set up, we know exactly how money flows through each cash register and it traces every measurable business function in our restaurants. We used to have to read every ticket to find out what people ate, how much their bill was, how many people were in their group. How many beers were sold today? How many glasses of chardonnay were consumed? What time do our employees come in? And how many customers did they turn over in one hour?

"Information like this is hitting the nail on the head. Food costing is another thing we know to the penny which helps us to buy wisely. Previously, I couldn't ask my book-keeper for information because she wouldn't have it until the end of the month. Now, we get to work every day and there's a printout on my desk that tells us what were the previous day's sales, the average ticket size, the five best sellers, the five worst sellers, the best waitresses of the day. It is amazing — for the tills come out exactly balanced every single day. We're no longer short, we're no longer over — it's fantastic. It's been great, and it gives us great control."

The threesome of mother, son and daughter have also accepted the challenge, as did Mo, of projecting Mo's to the world as a contributor to the communities their restaurants serve — in the tradition of the founder.

"We don't have a good business without a strong community," Cindy says. "We don't have a strong community without business being healthy and giving back to the community. That is our number one philosophy. If Mo came back today, she would be really happy. She would be right at home, except she would be annoyed with our no smoking policy."

How do you put a period at the end of a person's life? I thought about this question for a long time and so did my kids. We decided that the final words Father Louis Rodakowski said at Mo's memorial are most fitting.

He is a Catholic priest and was one of Granny's longtime friends. At the Newport Elks Lodge in February of 1992, he looked out at the crowded room, and told the mourners that he knew Mo was not religious, still he felt it was appropriate to wear his vestments in respect for his friend. He had no use, he said, for those who hid mean and hurtful hearts beneath their religion. "Mo Niemi," Father "Rod" told the crowd, "was genuine," adding, "I'll take a good person over a religious one, every time."

Chapter Five

There is one more chapter to Granny's story that confirms her philosophy of living and working in a way that proved utterly surprising to me.

The first hint of this surprise — an honor about to be bestowed on me — came one morning in April. I arrived for work at Mo's Annex with my head swirling with a hundred details for planning my daughter Gabrielle's wedding on May 19th. It was an ambitious undertaking, converting the Lincoln County Fair Grounds in Newport, Oregon, into chapel and reception site for the joyous occasion. We had decided to create a bright and colorful Mexican Fiesta for the more than 500 guests who would attend. I was totally immersed in my mother-of-the-bride mode, hell bent on getting the Mariachi band booked, and nothing was going to get in my way. But before I could get into my office, Gabrielle stopped me with a strange expression on her face.

"Mom," she said haltingly, "something really great has happened. You have been selected the Business Person of the Year for Oregon by the Small Business

Administration. I guess the timing is a bit tight what with the wedding and all — but, isn't it exciting?" Her eyes sparkled.

"You're kidding me. How'd I do that?" I managed to say.

Cindy receives Small Business Administration
Business of the Year Award in 2001.

Gabrielle laughed and said that she hadn't planned on telling me yet, because the Oregon SBA Award Banquet was not scheduled until after the national convention in Washington, D.C. The celebration would take place at the Portland Hilton on May 16.

"Oh, Mom, that's not all," Gabrielle gushed, hardly able to contain herself. But she couldn't hold back any longer. "You have also been chosen as one of the four national finalists for Small Business Person of the Year in the whole United States. And," she paused dramatically, "you'll be going to Washington, D.C. and to the White House in just a week."

I was speechless. I couldn't believe my ears. My daughter, behind my back, had written and then submitted a ten-page application to the Small Business Administration, and contacted a number business owners, bankers and heads of service organizations.

"Mom." she said, " I just wanted you to receive some kind of recognition for all the wonderful things you do for your employees and the community. I didn't realize it would be this big."

My head was spinning. Thoughts were racing around uncontrollably, leaving me jittery. The wedding! Gabrielle!

First things first, I decided quickly. The Mariachi band would have to wait. Now that the cat was out of the bag, the phone started ringing off the hook. A couple of TV stations wanted to interview me for their local business reports. Newspaper reporters wanted to see me. People called to congratulate me, and then, on top of it all, there came a call from the White House. *The White House!* Incredible! I was on the phone with a member of the White House staff, one of those people close to the President of the United States.

A pleasant male voice informed me that two White House staff members wanted to meet my family and me, and get a close look at the business that was about to receive a national award. We were being "checked out" by order of President Bush.

The next morning, at nine on the dot, two nice young men from Washington D.C. showed up at my office, settled in with cups of coffee and started to ask me questions. I guess they had to find out if indeed I was "for real," and if there was in fact a thriving, well established business. Also, in a subtle way they were feeling me out about my political leanings and to make sure I was not a malcontent.

With that part of the questioning out of the way, my visitors proceeded to tell me what lay ahead and for what I should be prepared. *The President wanted to meet all the finalists.* I felt small and insignificant compared to the magnitude and prestige of the honor I was about to receive. I kept thinking, "What did I do that was so special? What made me stand out? I was just doing my job. I was doing Mo's job. Is this really happening?"

Then I wondered how Granny would have responded? Knowing her as well as I did, she would have probably taken a big drag of her ever-present cigarette, blown out the smoke through her nose and and hollered a hearty, "Goddamn it, Cindy, you deserve it. Now go and have fun!"

I felt good about that for a moment or two, but then my mind returned to its wild jigs and cartwheels just thinking about the prospect of meeting President Bush. How many Americans get to meet the man in the White House? Would I have to talk to him? What would I say? My God, I'll be a blithering idiot, a virtual rainman. I thought how a year or two in Toastmasters would have come in handy at this point. I couldn't stop the flood of thoughts, and I was convinced that I'd be a total embarrassment to Oregon and my family.

I better not go, I decided. I'll just work on my daughter's wedding and be Cindy McEntee, owner of a little joint on Newport's waterfront in quiet, remote Oregon, and watch some well deserving, hard working business owner make us all proud. Stay home! How comforting, I thought.

Of course I'll go. Mo wouldn't have stewed or hesitated for a second. She would have loved to see herself celebrated, to make news, to see her name in print, pictured shaking hands with the President of the United States and walk away with a coveted national award. It would have been right up her alley.

I'll go. But what should I wear? How about my hair? I'll need a manicure. What to say? What? What? What? Typical stage fright thoughts were riding herd on my mind and I had to get on with business. So much for panicking. Time to accept this great moment, to get going and let the chips fall where they may.

Soon my entourage was forming: husband Bruce, daughter Gabrielle, son, Dylan, his wife Celeste, and my good friend and marathon partner, Jan Becker. We managed to purchase our airline tickets at a fabulous bargain price and made reservations at the Renaissance Hotel in Washington, D.C.

What I didn't know at the time was the "underhanded" role Gabrielle had played in getting the ball rolling for my recognition as an outstanding business woman. Not one word ever escaped from her to betray her plan for my national acclaim. And after it was all over, I had to congratulate myself for raising a daughter who could make such a fantastic thing happen, never once letting on how proud she was of her mother — not once taking credit for dreaming up the idea and doing all the preparatory work to contact the people who would help make it come true.

Finally, I learned how Gabrielle started her campaign. According to her, she said to Guy Faust at the Oregon Coast Community College, "I'd like to get some big recognition for my mother and what she does in the community."

"That's exactly what I said. And how do you to that? Guy handed me some papers and said, 'Here's an application. Submit this to the Small Business Administration, and see what happens.' It was ten pages of stuff that I had to fill out. Number one item was the history of Mo's, how she started, grew the business and what my mother is and why she should get this award.

"Then I had to call Fred Postalwaite and Dick Beamer: these people are big members of the community, movers and shakers who have helped change the community for the best.

"'Would you write my mother a letter of recommendation for this award.'

"And they did, of course.

"It was a big secret. I sat in the office and typed away like crazy and Mom thought I was really working hard. Then I received a call from the SBA and I was informed, 'Oh, yes, your mom is definitely Small Business Person of the Year in Oregon.

"Then, I almost jumped out of my chair, when the man I was talking to said, 'But here's the deal. She's also one of the four runner ups for the Small Business Person of the Year for the whole United States.'

"Oh my God, she'll kill me I thought, because I had put so many hours in to getting her honored. Then, the penny dropped and all of a sudden the Rotary called Mom and announced, 'We want you to be our Business Enterprise Winner of the Year.' And the Chamber of Commerce notified her that she was their Business Person of the Year. And it all happened in 2001.

"It was pretty cool, and I was so proud because she is so modest compared to what she has acomplished.

On the cover of *Inkfish Magazine,*
Gabrielle, Cindy and Dylan.

Receiving Austin Family Business Award "Women Owned
Business" — Oregon State University.
Dolores Austin, Bruce McEntee, Cindy, Gabrielle, Judy
and Bill Dixon, Mo's youngest son and wife.

I tried to get her to go to a fund-raiser one night, but she didn't want anybody to know about her and who she was. I remember saying, 'Mom we can't do this any more. This is a great business and it's great because of you. Because you do it all, and so expertly.' Maybe I'm more like Mo, I told her because I love the limelight. I'm going to push you into it."

Things were moving so fast that there was no time to bask in the glow of being the recipient of a national honor, nor to be fully aware and to enjoy the excitement of this once-in-a-life-time moment. In order to keep my emotional balance on a less helter-skelter keel until it was time to leave, I kept working on my daughter's wedding and put the upcoming trip east out of my mind's reach for a few moments.

Anticipation and excitement didn't really take hold of me until we boarded the plane for Washington. Thanks to Jan's husband, John, there was a limo that picked us up at the Baltimore Airport to take us on a scenic tour of our nation's capital. Our driver was accommodating and gave his carload of passengers some good pointers and suggestions on places to go and things to see. It was an odd feeling to be in the capitol of the United States where so many things that affected our lives were decided. How exciting! We drove by Arlington National Cemetery, got a good look at the Lincoln Memorial and off in the distance appeared the Washington Monument and the Capitol Building. Wow! Washington D.C. — where the history of our great nation is documented in marble and stone, and lives on to challenge the future. And I was part of it all.

After we arrived at our hotel and settled in, we were asked to serve Mo's Clam Chowder at a 'Best Of Business 2001 Showcase' scheduled for six o'clock that evening at the Hotel Renaissance. Thank God the kids had come along. They handled the task with great efficiency and aplomb. All I had to do was to show up. And show up I did in spite of all my trepidation and anxiety.

It was fun and interesting to meet the other candidates who had assembled for the award ceremony, even though it was a bit intimidating. There were so many qualified and deserving business owners whose companies had performed so well that I was wondering what I was doing among them.

But it was a great night. John Whitmore, acting administrator of SBA, handed out the awards to each individual chosen for the Small Business Person of the Year for his or her state. People cheered, hugged, applauded and congratulated each other. And while friends and family members watched, the winners had their photos taken with Mr. Whitmore proudly clutching the beautiful marble awards and, of course, I was among them.

The nominees' ride to the White House and the meeting with President Bush was scheduled for two o'clock in the afternoon on May 8th. Although all the activities of the two days led up to that moment, I still was shaking my head in wonder, and could not banish the feeling of floating in a dream. When I'd wake up, I would probably find myself having a cup of hot chowder at Mo's Annex, looking out at Yaquina Bay, during my lunch break. That's how unreal and unbelievable the whole thing was to me.

I was told that the White House ceremony was restricted to the nominees and their spouses, however, because I had placed in the top four, Gabrielle and Dylan were invited to attend. What a thrill it was for them. Sadly, Celeste and Jan remained at the hotel.

We climbed into a chartered bus that took us to the White House. After a fairly thorough security check, we followed our guide down a hallway, past the Rose Garden, into what is referred to as the "People's Room" and looked for a seat that would offer the best view of the event. Apparently ours was the last bus to arrive and seating was sparse, with mostly singles left in the back of the room.

But to my surprise and delight, I was directed to a front row seat with Bruce being seated directly behind me. The kids were escorted to the other side of the room with a good view of the happenings.

Once seated, a pall came over me and for a moment I froze: I'm sitting in the White House waiting for the President of the United States, the *Actual President in person!* Good God! I was pinching myself, this was truly a big day for me and my family. I looked over at Dylan and Gabrielle. They were doing the same thing I was — gawking at the room, admiring the ornate walls, taking in the people, the TV cameras, the view out the windows, the very sober young colonel who was directing things and keeping order. Finally, their eyes came to rest on the dais from where the President had delivered so many speeches to the nation. This was the very room where he greeted heads of state, dignitaries and distinguished visitors from all over the world.

This was by far the most surreal experience that had ever happened to me. Excitement and anticipation hovered over the crowded room like a cloud. I could hear my heart beat.

Suddenly, the young colonel appeared at our side and handed each finalist a note with instructions on what to say and how to act when President Bush arrived. It described how to approach him when he called out each individual name, the proper way to leave the podium area, and after that, what each of us should say to the crowd.

That's when I started to lose some of my composure. I was not prepared, or had expected, to address the crowd, face fifty TV cameras and God only knows how many reporters. All I could think of was … RAINMAN. Suddenly I realized that my hands were sweating — which had never happened to me before.

The President of the United States of America is going to shake my hand, my wringing-wet hand. How embarrassing! I want to go home! I turned around to look at Bruce for support and assurance. He was doing the same thing — mouth opened with awe and eyes glinting with a suspicious hint of moisture.

That got me. I was getting teary, and on top of that, I began to perspire. Time seemed to have stopped. Where is that guy? By the time he shows up I'll be dead from hyperventilation, maybe a heart attack or just drowning in my own sweat.

The moment finally arrived. A voice over a loudspeaker spoke the famous words that for more than two hundred years had brought countless people to their feet: "Ladies and Gentlemen, The President of the United States."

Still in a daze, I stood up with the others as the huge doors at the back of the room opened and there he was — the President of the United States. He walked briskly to the lectern — big smile, shaking hands as he walked up the aisle and took his place behind the podium. He was as big as life itself — the person who had just five months earlier taken on the job of running the most powerful nation in the world.

What the heck, I attempted to calm myself — he's just a guy. A guy from Texas. Yeah! But he *is* the President. Wow!

My heart skipped a beat or two. He looked pretty good, you know, not shorter or taller than I expected, just very approachable, with that little smirk across his face we have all seen. He really doesn't look that scary, but I still wished I could go to the bathroom or somewhere to get a little air. Instead, I took a deep breath and tried to relax. He acknowledged the thunderous applause, smiled, raised his hand and the room fell silent.

President Bush started the ceremony by delivering a short speech citing the tremendous value that small businesses of America are to the economy of the country. It was very difficult for me to remember exactly what he said. There was so much going on inside of me that honestly I didn't hear a word he said. I just watched his lips move, found myself joining in the enthusiastic applause of his audience, thinking that it must have been a compelling speech.

When the time came for the awards to be announced, the President started right out with the name: "*Christy* McEntee." What did he say? Who is Christy McEntee ? Jeeeezuuz, my name is CINDY! CINDY MCENTEE! Oh my God this was hysterical. Here was my big moment and I'm CHRISTY McEntee? I almost started laughing. Just what I needed, a round of hysterical giggles to relieve the stranglehold on my emotions.

This was FUNNY I have never forgotten that moment.

The moment passed, and I went back to stewing about the fact that the winner had to address the crowd. I don't want to be the winner, please. Panic. I should have stayed home, and I held my breath as the President announced the third runner up, and it was not *Christie* McEntee. Then he announced the second runner up and it was not me. At this point I really wanted time out to go to the powder room.

The President's voice hit my ears: "First runner up is CINDY MCENTEE." In a semi-trance accompanied by the heavy pounding of my fast-beating heart, I walked up to the podium and stood next to the President. Wow!

Someone took pictures, and we shook hands. President Bush talked to me the whole time I was at his side.

Cindy meets President Bush and wins
National Small Business Administration
First Runner Up Business of the Year.

"Hello Cindy," he greeted me. "You've done a wonderful job. I'm very proud to meet you. Now don't be nervous, just smile, you never know which camera is going to get our picture, and they are all taking them, you know. I hope you enjoy Washington while you're here."

He was probably wondering how I managed to run a successful business, worthy of the nation's top honor with so little command of the English language. I did manage a shaky, "Thank you, Mr. President, I appreciate your kind words." I knew he was probably used to people being in awe and rendered speechless by being in his presence.

In parting, the President turned to me and said, " It is a pleasure to meet you Ms McEntee. Keep up the good work."

Off I went back to my seat, clutching the trophy. For the remainder of the ceremony I sat stunned and shaken, but feeling incredibly honored and proud, convinced the event would always head the top of the "major events list" of my life.

After the awards had been given out, a reporter from Oregon approached me and asked: "Were you disappointed not winning?"

I was taken back by that foolish question, and with a sharp ring in my voice, I told the man, "It never occurred to me that I didn't win. I believe I won plenty!"

There were many wonderful experiences during the few but exciting days I stayed in Washington with my family, but none so indescribable as coming face to face with the President of the United States, receiving a coveted national award and to shake his hand.

No matter whether you agree with the politics of the man, whether you voted for him, or whether or not you like him, at a moment like that all personal thoughts take flight as you are aware of the power of the office, the power of the President of the United States and the magic of being in the White House — the place where history is made every moment of the day.

Mo would have loved it. She would have eaten it up. She would have basked in the glory of this proud moment. She would have made history, and she did through me.

From the depths of my heart, full of emotions, I addressed Mo as I often did in my private mind: "This award is for you, Granny. You started it all. You made it happen. You gave me wings to fly and the opportunity to follow in your footsteps. You trusted me with your dream. Thank you, Granny, I love you."